FROM WRITERS TO STUDENTS:
The Pleasures and Pains of Writing

Edited by
M. Jerry Weiss
Jersey City State College

For the
IRA Literature for Adolescents Committee

INTERNATIONAL READING ASSOCIATION
800 Barksdale Road • Newark, Delaware 19711

INTERNATIONAL READING ASSOCIATION

Copyright 1979 by the
International Reading Association, Inc.

Library of Congress Cataloging in Publication Data
Main entry under title:
  From writers to students.

  1. Children's literature—Authorship. 2. Children's literature, American—History and criticism. 3. Authors, American—20th century—Interviews. I. Weiss, Morton Jerome. II. International Reading Association. Literature for Adolescents Committee.
PN147.5.F7   808'.068   79-11695
ISBN 0-87207-724-1

CONTENTS

IRA Literature for Adolescents Committee

Ethna Reid, Board Liaison
Exemplary Center for Reading Instruction

M. Jerry Weiss, Chairperson
Jersey City State College

Patricia Allen
Harper and Row

Robert O. Boord
University of Nevada-Las Vegas

Dorothy Briley
Lothrop, Lee, and Shepard

Patricia Cianciolo
Michigan State University

Louis J. Clerico
Montclair (N.J.) Board of Education

Suzanne M. Coil
Avon Books, Inc.

Roger Cooper
Bantam Books, Inc.

Evelyn Diggs
Combined Book Exhibit, Inc.

Ken Donelson
Arizona State University

Betsy S. Gould
Dell Publishing Company

M. Jean Greenlaw
North Texas State University

Ava Grodner
Montclair (N.J.) High School

Emily Howard
William Morrow, Inc.

Paul B. Janeczko
Gray-Gloucester High School (Mass.)

Gillian Jolis
Ballantine Books, Inc.

Donald B. Reynolds, Jr.
Denver Public Schools

Shelton L. Root, Jr.
University of Georgia

Peter L. Sanders
Wayne State University

Maria Schantz
Montclair State College

Deon O. Stevens
University of Utah

Jean Neville Webster
Laurenvale School Board
Quebec, Canada

The Committee gratefully acknowledges the assistance of the following members of the Jersey City State College administrative staff:

Joseph W. Drew, Vice President for Academic Affairs
Sydelle Kirschbrown, Duplicating Services
Lee Krieg, Secretarial Assistance
Jack List, Director of Business Services
Lucille McCarthy, Secretarial Assistance
Edwin G. Weisman, Vice President, Business and Finance

iv

PREFACE

Writers on Writing

What is a writer? How do writers feel about writing? How does one become a writer? Is it worth it?

So many students have raised these questions, and so many adults are concerned about levels of literacy today, the International Reading Association Committee on Adolescent Literature decided to find some answers to these questions. Successful writers reach readers. How? What impact does reading make upon the reader? Do readers aspire to become writers?

This volume has tapped some of the most talented and generous persons in publishing and education.

The members of the Committee on Adolescent Literature feel this monograph will offer insights and inspiration beneficial for promoting a love and respect for reading and writing.

This two-year project is just a beginning. Let IRA hear from you. What other questions are in your minds? Together we may find answers for motivation and success.

MJW

The interviews in this volume are available on cassette tapes. For information and prices, write to the Order Department, IRA, 800 Barksdale Road, P.O. Box 8139, Newark, Delaware 19711.

INTRODUCTION

What's in Adolescent Books for Me?

That's a good question, and I'd like to take a shot at answering it. Over the years, some teachers, librarians, parents, and young people have made fun of books written for young people. They argued that plots in adolescent literature were uncomplicated, unrealistic, and childish; characterizations were sketchy, obvious, and stereotyped; values were preached rather than implied and were consistently white and middle-class; themes were condescending and simple-minded, and endings of the books were inevitably and unrealistically happy with good guys always winning out and bad guys getting their just desserts. Sometimes, they argued that taboos forbidding the mentioning of pregnancy, drugs, divorce, death, sexuality, sensuality, school dropouts, profanity, or racial tensions made adolescent books all sweetness and light and hopelessly out of touch with the real world and automatically fifth-rate literature at best.

Those arguments were convincing, given the kinds of adolescent books published in the 1950s and early 1960s. Only a book here or there provided an exception. Books with titles like *Sheri's First Dance, A Touchdown for Jefferson High, Jeannie Joins a Sorority, Canadian Road Race, Pirates of the South Seas,* or *Isabelle, Young Reporter* did little to challenge readers or connect with reality.

Some adults and young people believe that nothing has changed and all these charges are still true. But adolescent books have changed greatly, some people would even say they've changed drastically, since about 1965 or so. Many adolescent books today are worthwhile. They are better written, are related to the real world, and no longer insult by talking down to or preaching at the reader.

Adolescent books today contain far more complex and believable plots. Characterizations reveal sometimes baffled or troubled young people searching for answers to confusing issues. Things don't always end happily or easily. The humor is more fun and hopeful and mature. Themes reflect problems of loneliness, alienation, death; questions about family or social values; and concerns about personal and sexual identity in today's world. Old taboos have

1

been eliminated, and books now treat almost any subject of concern to adolescents.

Not all adolescent books today are great stuff. Many of them are as old-fashioned as the titles I mentioned earlier. Some books aren't about real people but instead are about problems young people have—some authors apparently pick something like pregnancy and write their "pregnancy" books or suicide and write their "suicide" books or drugs or abortion or mental illness or family fights or politics. I guess we shouldn't be surprised since adult writers do the same things *if* they care more about the problems (or making money) than they do about trying to do something far more important and far more difficult, namely, writing an honest story about people caught up in real problems and trying to find a way out. That doesn't mean that everything ought to be deadly serious in that honest book, but only that the author ought to take his ideas and readers seriously.

And a number of authors of adolescent books take themselves seriously. Let me mention just a few authors and titles I think you would like. I'm going to put them under four categories of modern adolescent literature, actually themes common to many adult and adolescent authors.

First, our essential and eternal loneliness, the feeling all of us get that we are alone in this big and awesome and cold world. We all need love and companionship and that's pointed up in books like Ronald Lockley's *Seal-Woman*, Katie Letcher Lyle's *Fair Day and Another Step Begun*, Robert Newton Peck's *A Day No Pigs Would Die* (if you really don't believe that adolescent books have anything to offer, this is a good place to begin to challenge that idea), M.E. Kerr's *If I Love You, Am I Trapped Forever?*, Mary Stolz's *Leap Before You Look*, S.E. Hinton's *The Outsiders*, or Paul Zindel's *The Pigman*.

Second, our need for laughter, the feeling that if we can't occasionally laugh we'll go mad. That's basic to books like M.E. Kerr's *Dinky Hocker Shoots Smack*, Bruce Clements' *I Tell a Lie Every So Often*, John Ney's *Ox: The Story of a Kid at the Top*, John Donovan's *Family*, Walter Dean Myers' *Fast Sam, Cool Clyde and Stuff*, Richard Peck's *The Ghost Belonged to Me*, or Paula Danziger's *The Cat Ate My Gymsuit*.

Third, our need for hope. With everything possible going wrong with the world (or maybe it just seems that way), we need to find hope, reassurance that maybe we'll survive, maybe we're even worth survival. We need books like Patricia McKillip's *The Forgotten Beasts of Eld*, Ellen Bridger's *Home Before Dark*, John Donovan's *Remove Protective Coating a Little at a Time*, Carol Farley's *The Garden Is Doing Fine*, Anne McCaffrey's *Dragonsong*, Ursula LeGuin's *Earthsea* trilogy, Sharon Bell Mathis' *Listen for the Fig Tree*, or Laurence Yep's *Sweetwater*.

Fourth, our need to question values, our need to wonder about everything and come to our decisions about ideas and what we choose to believe in, what we need to believe in. Books like these may help: Robert Cormier's *The*

Chocolate War or *I Am the Cheese*, Robert McKay's *Skean*, Honor Arundel's *The Blanket Word*, Isabelle Holland's *The Man without a Face*, Rosa Guy's *Ruby*, Mildred Lee's *Fog*, Norma Fox Mazer's *A Figure of Speech*, or Nicholasa Mohr's *Nilda*.

I haven't listed all the writers I think you'd enjoy reading, but you get the idea. Adolescent literature may not yet be everything it ought to be, but it has taken some giant steps in the past few years toward becoming honest literature about real people engaged in trying to find some answers to very real dilemmas. That's what literature is all about, whether it's adolescent or adult literature. In the long run, that's why I think you'd enjoy reading some of these books, not because they're written for you but because they're written about you and you can find yourself (and other people you know) in them. Even better, you just might find some hope and humor and answers.

KEN DONELSON

AUTHOR INTERVIEWS

SUE ALEXANDER

Interviewed by M. Jerry Weiss

BOOKS BY SUE ALEXANDER

Peacocks Are Very Special   Doubleday
Small Plays for Special Days   Seabury
Small Plays for You and A Friend   Seabury (Scholastic Book Service)
Witch, Goblin, and Sometimes Ghost   Pantheon

J.W. It's a pleasure to introduce Sue Alexander who has written *Witch, Goblin, and Sometimes Ghost; Peacocks Are Very Special;* and *Small Plays for You and A Friend,* among others. Sue, welcome. I'd like to begin by asking you how and when did you decide to become a writer?

S.A. I don't know that I ever really decided to become a writer. I've been writing stories since I was eight years old. I'll tell you how I began writing stories. I'm very small (four feet ten); when I was eight years old, I was much smaller. I was the smallest person in my class and I was very clumsy. I couldn't walk down the hall without tripping over my own feet. Consequently, the kids in my class didn't want to play with me at recess time because I was so clumsy I ruined the games; so I sat by myself. Then one day I was very sick and tired of sitting by myself. There was a boy who wasn't playing either, and I said, "Come on; I'll tell you a story." And I began to tell a story that I made up as I went along. Before I was finished with the story, all the rest of the class had come to listen. It made me feel good and I figured, this is the way I'm going to have company every recess. And, after a few days of telling stories, I realized that if I stopped at a certain point, they would all say, "What happened next?" And I could say, "Well, come back tomorrow." So I began to write the stories down. After that, I wrote for myself, stories that I needed to tell myself to make my world come right. Then I wrote stories when I was a mother to tell my children. I never thought, really, of becoming a professional writer until, I guess, my youngest child was three. All of a sudden, one day, I said, "Well, why don't I try to sell some of what I write?" And so I tried, and discovered that there's a great deal of craft involved. There's a big difference in telling stories for yourself or your children and telling stories that go in books; and I set out to learn the craft.

J.W. How did you learn it?

S.A. Trial and error, for the most part. The only way you can learn to write is to write, to keep trying, and to read. I did. I still read. I've always read. I read and I wrote—I wrote thousands of words of stories that never got anywhere. I don't regret any one of them; they helped me to learn.

J.W. How did your first book get published?

S.A. My first book is *Small Plays for You and A Friend.* After I'd sold some stories (I didn't know why those stories sold and others that I had out at different publishers hadn't sold), I went to a writer's conference and I met Mary Elting and Franklin Folsom, two marvelous writers. I showed them my manuscripts and said, "Tell me why these sold and these did not; maybe, if I understand, I can know what I'm doing." They sat down with my manuscripts and we talked. They explained to me that what I'd done in the stories that had sold was that I'd lived inside the children I'd written about. In the stories that had not sold, I had been looking at them from the outside. I began to understand then how I had to operate as a writer—to get inside my characters, because I could remember being inside the characters in the stories that had sold. Then they said to me, "Some of the stories haven't sold because they're not magazine stories; they're books and you've been sending them to the wrong market." They suggested I send them to Beatrice De Regniers who, besides being a very talented writer, is an editor at *Scholastic.* So I started sending stories to her and with each one she rejected, she sent me a long letter and invited me to submit more. I did; and one day, when my daughter was about seven, she said to me, "I can't find any plays just for me and my friend." We went to the library and we found plays for thirty kids, six kids, twelve kids, but not two kids. That night, I sat down and wrote four plays for her and her girlfriend. After I'd written them and they'd played them for me and my husband, I took another look at the plays and said to myself, "If they've enjoyed them so, wouldn't other children?" So I polished them and straightened them out a little bit and sent them off. And that became my first book.

J.W. Do you find today, as you write, that you have to rewrite much of your material after its conception and first draft?

S.A. Always. I don't think I've ever written one draft only. I don't think that's possible. Perhaps it is for some people; for me, it is absolutely impossible. I write my first draft in longhand. My mind goes too fast to work on a typewriter. Where I don't know the right word or the right name—because names are very important—I make straight lines. Then I go back and my second and subsequent drafts (at times there are twenty and thirty drafts or more) are done on a typewriter because then I have to see it and I have to hear it in that inner ear in my head. It has to have a rhythm—not rhyme—but a rhythm. The rhythm of the telling is so important to me and I have to find the right word to give it that rhythm and the right sentences and the right mood—until it all comes together. It's never the first; the first draft is getting it down before it gets away—getting down the intenseness of the emotion that I feel as I'm writing. Then, the other drafts are the craft part of my work.

J.W. Do you find brief writing to be a difficult task for you?

S.A. Writing is very difficult. It is also the most enjoyable thing in the world, even when I'm crying because the right words won't come. I wouldn't trade it for anything else. There's nothing that makes me happier than when I'm writing. There's no joy to surpass getting an emotion down on paper so that it can be communicated to other people.

J.W. Where did you find *Witch, Goblin, and Sometimes Ghost?*

S.A. I don't know whether I can really go all the way back. I've been living with goblins so long. *Goblin* originated, to the best of my memory, out of my feeling that it simply wasn't fair that kids didn't understand sometimes that everybody else felt the same way they felt about a lot of things. One day I found myself listening to Goblin, and I kept trying to find a story home for him—the right story for him, and I couldn't. But I liked him and he spoke to me and he meant a great deal to me. Through the years I kept trying. After the first couple of years, he was joined by Witch and Ghost. I was listening to their conversations for years, trying to get them down; and it wasn't right until one day I tried to put them in the format that they are in now and that fit them exactly right. The short sentences were able to convey their feelings and their actions—to have the rhythm in which I knew their stories had to be told. It was a day of great joy for me when I started to write them in that format.

J.W. You have created characters with tremendous emotion—happy, sad, suspenseful. Do you think that the modern writer is committed to message-telling through his stories?

S.A. I hope not! Part of the thing that's on my mind, and I hope on most writers' minds, is to tell a story. I have a compelling need to tell a story. If you're a person who has values, your values are going to come through in the story—that's apparent. It's been said, "You are what you write, and you write what you are," and there's no getting away from it. That's exactly what happens.

J.W. Do you think that television and movies have influenced you as a writer in any way, shape, or form?

S.A. I think that everything that happens to a person throughout his life, every experience he has, whether it's a visual experience, a reading experience, or a living experience, influences him in some way. It makes its mark. I think that's impossible to get away from. How much influence, or where, I don't think any of us is conscious of; at least I am not. I know I'm conscious of reading always and wishing that I could write prose that sings as some prose that I have read. I don't know if I'll ever be able to.

J.W. Who are some of these writers that you admire?

S.A. Jane Yolen, for one. Her writing just sings. It's more poetry than prose; it's prose—but its poetry. It's beautiful and it's moving. Julia Cunningham, for another. Her writing is haunting. There are so many. I'd have to say Arnold Lobel. I think the man is a genius. I come to books, I suppose, rather naively and uncritically. I am prepared to enjoy and be in love with each and every one. I'm disappointed when I'm not, when that doesn't happen. But I come to them with a feeling of delightful anticipation.

J.W. I love that statement that you come naively and not too critical-ly. I think critics seem to dictate in the publishing field to a large extent as to what makes it and what doesn't. Do you find critics to be important to a writer?

S.A. Well, I'd have to say they are important, undoubtedly, to the sale of books, but they are not important to the writer in the writing. They have nothing to do with it. That's always after the fact. Certainly, as a writer for children, you know that there are certain critical media that determine whether your books are ever going to reach children and so you're conscious of them, but always after the fact. They have nothing to do with the writing. I don't care what the critics say; I have to write what I have to write. If they choose not to like it, that is up to them. I can't do anything about it. I must do what I must do. Certainly, I hope that my books will reach children, but I can't worry about that while I'm writing.

J.W.   Do you think that schools or teachers or librarians in your own life influenced you to become a writer?

S.A.   No, not really. As I grew up writing, it was for myself; it was a very private thing. It never would have occurred to me to discuss it with a teacher or a librarian. Certainly, I had teachers and librarians who shared my love of books and with whom I could talk about the books I loved. But it never occurred to me to tell them that I was writing anything. It was very private. I honestly can't say that they influenced me in any way, because I don't know that I chose to be a writer; I think it was kind of inevitable. It is my life. I need to write as I need to breathe. I'm desperately unhappy when I'm not writing.

J.W.   If you could give any brief advice to someone who would want to become a writer, what might you suggest?

S.A.   Read and read and read and read. Read everything and anything you can get your hands on; and then write. And rewrite. And write again, because those are the only ways. There is nothing else. You learn from the books; you learn the rhythm of the language and you learn how it sounds in your head. Write it down and it's not right the first time. You write it again and it's still not right. You write it again and again until it says exactly what you want to say in the way you want to say it. There's no substitute for reading and there's no substitute for writing. If you want to write, you have to do both. Those are the only pieces of advice I can give anybody.

J.W.   Are you working on another writing project at the present time?

S.A.   I'm always working on another writing project. At the moment, I'm writing another book about Goblin, other stories about Goblin and his friends. I'm having a good time. I like Goblin and he likes me. We talk together, in the beginning, at this point; but I've been looking forward to telling more stories about Goblin.

J.W.   This brings up an interesting point: Some writers have commented that writing books in which characters are followed through in a series may have a more difficult time in being published than a book with new characters and new events or situations. Do you feel that is true?

S.A. I don't know that I've ever thought about it, really, because at the time that I wrote the Goblin stories, there were other stories about Goblin that I wanted to do, but they could not fit in one book. My editor knew that. But, in between, I have written other things, told other stories, because stories don't happen overnight. I can't sit down at my desk and say "Today I'm going to write a story about Goblin." It doesn't work that way. Goblin talks to me in my head for a long time before I write anything down. And that happens with every kind of book.

J.W. Have any of your readers' responses had any influence on you as a writer?

S.A. Only sheer delight, very honestly. I love hearing from my readers. That gives me the greatest joy that there is. The first letter that I got from a reader, I sat and cried all day. I wrote back to the little girl and told her it was the first letter I'd gotten from someone who had read my book and that it made it very special. Her letter hangs on the wall near my desk, so I can look at it. They're very special; they say to me that I have touched somebody's heart and that's a very special feeling. They are not—or have not been as yet—critical letters in the sense that they wish I had done this or that; they are telling me how they feel about the characters that I've written about. Even if it's not how I saw the characters, the characters have touched the readers somehow, and it makes me feel just marvelous.

J.W. Well, you've summarized pretty well what a successful writer is and that you've touched somebody and you have the opportunity to hear about that emotional contact. You have contributed very much to the wonderful world of reading and writing, books and readers. We thank you very much for taking the time to talk with us.

JUDY BLUME

Interviewed by M. Jerry Weiss

BOOKS BY JUDY BLUME

Are You There, God? It's Me, Margaret   Bradbury
   (Dell)
Blubber   Bradbury Press (Dell)
Deenie   Bradbury Press (Dell)
Forever   (Pocket Books)
Freckle Juice   (Scholastic Book Services)
Iggie's House   Bradbury Press (Dell)
It's Not the End of the World   Bradbury Press
   (Bantam)
Otherwise Known As Sheila the Great   Dutton (Dell)
Starring Sally J. Freedman as Herself   Bradbury Press
   (Dell)
Tales of a Fourth Grade Nothing   Dutton (Dell)
Then Again Maybe I Won't   Bradbury Press (Dell)

J.W.   Hello. I'm M. Jerry Weiss, and it's my pleasure to interview Judy
Blume, author of such books as *Are You There, God? It's Me,
Margaret; Blubber; Tales of a Fourth Grade Nothing;* and *Deenie.*
Judy, how and when did you decide to become a writer?

J.B.   That's a difficult question. I think it goes back to me as a kid
making up stories in my head—not sharing them and not writing them
down but, certainly, always having a movie inside my head. Then, when
I had my own young children and wanted a career very much, but didn't
want to go back into classroom teaching because I wanted to be home
with them for awhile, it just seemed the natural thing to do—to write
down some of my stories.

Judy Blume

J.W. Where did these stories come from? Where do you get your ideas?

J.B. Well, a lot of them come because I have this wonderful memory; so I write a lot out of the child I was; and then because I live with two children, I get other ideas from them. And from things I read and see and people I meet. I'm not sure, too much, how it works and it's a scary thought to think about, so I just let it happen. I always know that another idea will come. *Deenie* was specific because I met a young girl— fourteeen years old—with scoliosis and she was willing to share some of her feelings with me. Then I talked to a lot of other scoliosis patients and their families; and I did research—I did go to the hospital and watch kids and talk to doctors. It was the only book for which I did basic research before I could write it.

J.W. Are your other books from your own family or your own experiences to a large extent? Or from people you've known?

J.B. Well, yes and no. I think you may start out basing it on something that you know well and then, with me anyhow, it grows as I put it on paper. The characters don't really live in my head; they come alive as I start to write about them; then I am never sure what is going to happen. I'm always surprised.

J.W. It must be fun.

J.B. Sometimes it's fun. The fun days are what keep me going. Most of the time it is not fun to write.

J.W. Writing is difficult?

J.B. Very difficult. I think what I hate most about it is the loneliness.

J.W. What do you mean? What kind of loneliness?

J.B. I like to be with people, and writing is a solitary life. It's you, alone, in a room with the typewriter.

J.W. I think your characters are filled with all of the emotions that people—children growing up—go through: the joyous side, the humorous side, the sad side. Is this intentional?

J.B. I am a very emotional person myself: I laugh a lot; I cry a lot; and I have a temper. I guess I really run the gamut, and I give in to my emotions. Maybe that's why I create emotional characters.

J.W. Do you think a writer has a responsibility to teach anything through her writing?

J.B. That is not something I think about, certainly, when I am doing a book. I think of myself more as one who reflects reality, paints a picture.

I would rather have my readers reach their own conclusions through their feelings than my batting them over the head.

J.W.   You've said on a number of occasions that truth and honesty and feeling....

J.B.   Yes, I do believe that one must, in my kind of books—or for me—present the truth; I must deal honestly. I think that's important.

J.W.   Do you think that any one of your books in particular reflects your life or the things you believe in more than any other book you have done?

J.B.   Certainly, my latest book, *Starring Sally J. Freedman as Herself*, is my most autobiographical book in that it is about the kind of imaginative child I was—very active fantasy life. And the family in that book is really very much my family. It is the first time I have ever dealt with my own family. I haven't felt ready. I have always known that I had this book inside me, that I had this story to tell; but I have never been able to do it until now.

J.W.   This is your latest. Are you working on another one now?

J.B.   I'm working on two: one is for young children and the other is an adult novel. Then I'll go back, when I've finished these, to a book about a thirteen- or fourteen-year-old.

J.W.   What advice would you give to someone who would like to be a writer?

J.B.   I don't think anyone can teach you to write. You write out of yourself. You write out of your own needs. The only advice I can offer, I think, is to write of what you know and what you care about. It doesn't have to be fact for fact; but I think, if you are dealing with fiction, in order to make it real, it has to be very real to you; and the way to make it real, at least in the beginning, is to deal with what you know, the feelings that you have experienced.

J.W.   When you write, have you ever tried your books out on young people to see how they respond?

J.B.   There is only one person who sees my book, from the first draft right through, and that is my daughter, Randy, who is now sixteen. She has always come home from school and picked up the latest pages—from the very, very rough first draft (I usually do three or four before it goes to my editor, and then I do a great deal of rewriting afterwards with my editor). Randy is the only person that I allow to read the first draft.

J.W. Have you had any delightful moments in having young people write to you about their reactions to your books?

J.B. Oh, yes. Years of delightful moments.

J.W. I can imagine that students identify and feel that you are a messiah because you seem to capture their feelings and concerns.

J.B. They certainly write very personal letters; and they often spill out their feelings to me because I'm real to them, and yet I'm not real. It's easier, I think, to deal with your innermost feelings when you're not connected with the other person.

J.W. Have there been any authors who have influenced you to write? Or influenced you as a writer? I imagine you're an avid reader and you enjoy reading.

J.B. When I first decided to try writing for young people, I went to the library and I came home with just cartons of books, day after day after day; and I would read them all and put them into categories of "These I Love," and "These Bore Me." Naturally, I wanted to write the kinds of books that I loved reading. *Harriet the Spy* was a very favorite of mine, and I tried to pay homage to *Harriet* and Louise Fitzhugh. At the end, I choke up and blubber when they're doing a Thanksgiving pageant and Jo wishes it would be like the one in *Harriet the Spy*. I love Elaine Koenigsberg's books and Beverly Cleary's books. These are books that really stand out in my mind. Then I was led to Marilyn Sachs' books, which I like very much. I think there is a certain amount of imitation in writing; but then you can stop worrying about that because, while there are only so many ideas floating around, when you're doing it word-for-word, by yourself, it's going to be yours.

J.W. I think you are unique in that you, more so than most writers, really get into these inner feelings. You certainly made people react who have read *Then Again, Maybe I Won't* and *Margaret* and *Iggie's House*. I think these must be tremendously rewarding experiences—to know that, inside of you, you have a way of being able to put these words down so carefully that readers everywhere identify with your talents.

J.B. Yes, but you don't know any of that when you're writing. And with each book that I write, I am just as insecure as I was with the first book. Maybe all writers are that insecure, I don't know; I'm a very poor judge of my own work while I'm doing it. The only clue I have as to whether a book is working is by asking "Am I enjoying it?" It seems to me that if it comes easily, once it starts to come, then it's going to be better than if it's a real struggle. That's when I know that things are going well for me. It's a good day because maybe ten pages will come out of it.

J.W. Once you have a book published and have the marvelous acclaim that you've had with your books, I imagine it's much easier to get books at least looked at and considered by publishers. Would you mind telling us if you had any difficulty at all in getting your first book published?

J.B. I had at least two and one-half years of constant rejection slips. The first one sent me into the closet and I cried and cried and cried. Then, after two and one-half years of it, you get a little harder; you don't cry so much over each rejection slip. On the other hand, what I wrote then wasn't very good, and I was learning, so I'm glad that none of them were published. And I never would have any of them published. I saved those early books to remind me how it was when I started.

J.W. Are there topics that you think young people are interested in reading about today that may not have been so in other times? Do you think your books seem to be pretty universal for all times?

J.B. I have no idea of what's going to happen with them; but, certainly, the topics that I've dealt with are topics that I would have been interested in myself when I was a kid. But there just weren't any books. I grew up on *Nancy Drew* and sneaking through my parents' bookshelves and finding choice passages here and there. Children's books just didn't deal with real life, what we were thinking or feeling, when I was a kid.

J.W. What are these things of "real life" that you think are so important for kids to find?

J.B. I think it's the same for everyone. I think all people want to read about themselves, want to say, "Oh, yes. I know, I understand. I know how she's feeling. I know how he's feeling." And that's pretty universal. I don't think it matters whether it's a kid's book or an adult's book.

J.W. They're filled with friendship, sexual awareness, growing up— these are issues, I think, that are so important in your life in terms of what you're trying to express. Is this true? Was that a fair appraisal?

J.B. I guess so. Yes, probably. I write about what's important to me, I suppose.

J.W. We're very fortunate in having Judy Blume, and I thank you very much for taking the time to chat with us.

J.B. Thank you, Jerry.

VERA and BILL CLEAVER
Interviewed by Alice Smith

BOOKS BY THE CLEAVERS

Delpha Green and Company   Lippincott (New American Library)
Dust of the Earth   Lippincott (New American Library)
Ellen Grae   Lippincott (New American Library)
Grover   Lippincott (New American Library)
I Would Rather Be a Turnip   Lippincott (New American Library)
Lady Ellen Grae   Lippincott (New American Library)
Me Too   Lippincott (New American Library)
The Mimosa Tree   Lippincott (New American Library
The Mock Revolt   Lippincott (New American Library)
Trial Valley   Lippincott (Bantam)
Where the Lillies Bloom   Lippincott (New American Library)
The Whys and Wherefores of Littabelle Lee   Atheneum (New American Library)

A.S.   The Cleavers have written twelve books for young readers and currently have another work in progress. While some are concerned with the literature for the young, the Cleavers' works have been termed regional, so I would like to begin this interview by asking Bill: Do you and Vera regard yourselves as regional writers?

B.C.   No, although the aspect is not unpleasing; possibly, it stems from our three Appalachian books, *Where the Lillies Bloom, The Mimosa Tree* and now, *Trial Valley*. For purposes of this discussion, let me pretend for a minute that I am a native southerner and that I don't entirely understand the term *regional*. Every corner of our land is regional. Each writer of fiction has his or her region. I suggest that the word regional is applied more often to the southern writer than to others because the south is less understood than other areas of our country. It is easy to understand a city because, in general, cities are pretty much alike. But in the hummocks, swamps, and hollows of the south there is still retained a slight air of mystery, of differences. By reason of his inherited environment, the southerner is softer, I think, than his northern cousins, and so his region presents, possibly, a naivete.

A.S. Now, the burial scene in *Where the Lillies Bloom* has been widely acclaimed, and yet there are some students and educators who still criticize that. Vera, what do you think about that?

V.C. Well, I think this brings us to another facet in the writing of fiction. The art of realism in fiction, which is truth, is what I am talking about. When the serious writer, wishing to give something of depth and value, approaches his fiction, I think it should be the aim to present situations and characters in the most realistic light possible, even if the situations are grotesque and the characters are nonstandard. In the most crucial interpretation, the fiction writer strives to see what he sees as truth. When Mary Call and Romey Luther buried their father on Old Joshua, they were being true to the conditions of their circumstances, aside from the fact that the Luther children moved in secrecy to protect themselves from the dangers of being sent to a care-home. They were also keeping a promise to their father. There was a fidelity to the situation to be exerted.

A.S. It's rather apparent to me. I felt it very strongly.

V.C. Yes, Alice, but we have been criticized by students from various universities around the country. They have written to us and asked us why we didn't give Roy a Christian burial; why did it have to be done in this manner? The question always surprises me because I thought it had been explained in the text of the work. But to get back to the question of why didn't we give the father, Roy, a decent Christian burial (the questioners call it a "decent Christian burial"). As creators of the situation, we could not say it is unChristian to bury the father in this manner; we must get an undertaker and a minister and give Roy Luther a proper Christian burial. There was no money for an undertaker or a minister. I am most aware that there are charitable ministers, but this

16   Vera and Bill Cleaver

was not the case in *Where the Lillies Bloom.* In this work the preacher, and I quote now, "has a mighty voice, but he expects to be paid for his wisdom," end of quote. So, to get back to the burial scene and the problem some people have with it—the situation was there and the circumstances were there and we, as writers, had to deal with the situation and its circumstances on its own terms. This is true in all my writing, and I think it should be true in all of fiction writing. If you have a situation, it has to be dealt with on the character's terms, not on the writer's terms.

A.S.   That's a criterion for all good writing, I think. Now, let's talk about the mechanics of writing for a moment; the actual production of it. What would you think are some of the most difficult aspects, Bill?

B.C.   They are all difficult; there's no quick and easy road. To entertain such a notion is folly and a waste of time. It's a pipe dream. Consider themes, just for a starter. Good themes are very hard to come by. We write for the young and there seems to be a notion that the young are not so perceptive as adults. Therefore, the slipshod books which present no outlook on life or any philosophy—slight stories which rush from motion to motion, which present no imagery, which do not ask the reader to pause and reflect—are thought to be acceptable to the juvenile and young adult.

A.S.   ·You don't do that because you don't write down to your audience.

B.C.   That's true.

V.C.   No, we don't write down to our audiences. We don't believe in altering a phrase or sentence in order to simplify for the sake of simplification alone. Nor do we address the thought held by some that children dodge unfamiliar words. I realize that there's a large opinion sweeping the country that our system of education is in serious trouble. It is in serious trouble because our young students are coming up to high school age, even to college levels, and they are not able to understand language as we know it. But to get back to our writing down to audiences, I keep bringing in here the serious writer. The serious writer is addicted to words, and while there are times when his first selection of words will turn out to be the best, this is rare. Sometimes Bill and I search for hours just for the right word and, even after we have selected and made a second or third selection of words, the next day we find that they are no good; so we have to discard and start all over again. I don't believe that there is any language capable of reflecting the entire human condition with all its problems. But because the writer has taken this on—and I'm talking about the human condition now as one of his personal responsibilities—he views the world as his personal problem; he continues to strive for the near-perfect in his choice of language. To move characters from scene to scene and situation to situation (I am again talking about the difficult mechanics of writing), to make it appear that this is done without effort is one of the trickiest, most time-consuming and frustrating points of writing. The dedicated writer will, I think, through the use of word choice, translate movements so the reader will not feel that he is being jerked along, but that he is being asked to view characters going from place to place and from situation to situation in a plausible way.

A.S. You do that very well. You also have been lauded for your originality. Do you write from experience or imagination? Or possibly both?

B.C. Well, both. I don't go along with the idea that a writer, in order to successfully present a work, must have lived that of which he writes. I should like to quote here a passage from an interview with Paul Green, a North Carolina writer. The question put to Mr. Green was, "Do you feel that being a southerner has its advantages for writing?" His answer was, "Yes, I think so. If raw experience is the first need, and maybe it is—experience linked with imagination (and here I hurry to say that there can be both kinds of experiences—the actual kind and the imaginative kind). Some of our writers have held the aesthetic credo that in order to write about an experience, one must have had that experience. Of course, this is nonsense. The author of *Crime and Punishment* did not have to go out and kill two old women in order to do it, and he wrote horrifyingly well. No, the purpose of the imagination is to be able to experience and see and feel, by proxy as it were." We agree with Mr. Green. We have not experienced all of which we write; some, yes, but not all. We have observed. You might say we are professional observers.

A.S. I notice in your works that you always present serious social conflicts. Do you think this is a necessary thing to do in writing for young readers?

V.C. Yes, it is for us. Without conflicts, fiction writing becomes essays; and conflict comes from a struggle between good and evil. A magazine which is distributed in our school system asked us to write three short stories. They offered a pretty good price, so I said, "We are not into any heavy work now; let's tackle this." So we sat down and wrote three short stories. They were unsuccessful because we were not tackling any serious themes. In fact, one of the rules of this little game was, they did not want a theme. So, my difficulty was I don't know how to write without a theme, whether it's a serious theme or an unserious theme. I simply don't know how anyone can sit down and write anything of value without a theme; I don't know how to do it.

A.S. How do you feel about that, Bill?

B.C. I feel that I should add here that we have never intentionally written a children's book in our life.

A.S. Oh, really?

B.C. That's right. *Ellen Grae*, our first published book back in 1967, was written in 1966 for a slick magazine, *McCall's*, I think. We had an agent then, and when they turned it down, our agent suggested we lengthen it and try to get it published as a juvenile book. We did that; we added about ten or fifteen thousand words and sent it in, and the first publisher who read it, bought it. Of course, not being in children's writing back in 1967, there were so many taboos that we knew nothing about. At that time, you couldn't write about divorce, drunkenness, and lots of other things. Today you can get away with almost anything. Well, not knowing about all the taboos, we broke a great number of them in *Ellen Grae*. It took some time for the controversy to die down, but by today's standards, *Ellen Grae* would be considered quite a square book.

A.S. In spite of that, did you know that *Ellen Grae* has been used by us in bibliotherapy?

B.C. Yes. We are recommended in almost every list we pick up, for this or that.

A.S. So it really can't be too square.

B.C. No, that's true. But, by Judy Blume's standards or Paul Zindel's, it is.

A.S. But you are your own type; you need to stick to something that is your own type; to your own self be true.

V.C. Let's discuss here for a moment this new permissiveness in children's literature. I don't believe in all-out permissiveness, to use street language. I don't go along with that. We were at West Virginia University several years ago attending an institute, and I made the statement then that one of the most tragic aspects of life, I think, is the inability of a person to stand on his own two feet. This is the theme that runs through all of our works, because Bill and I are strong people. Neither of us was born with a golden spoon in his mouth; we both came from the wrong side of the tracks. We have had to educate ourselves and do all sorts of things, as people of our era coming up during the depression had to do.

A.S. I think you are hitting the point, though.

B.C. I wasn't going to say much, but along those same lines, the war came along about the time my education should have started, and I went into World War II.

A.S. You mean your higher education.

B.C. Yes, that's what I mean.

V.C. I didn't have any higher education.

B.C. I didn't either. In fact, we both admit, even on our book jackets, that we were educated by libraries, the public libraries of the United States, but it just took thirty years longer than most people spend.

A.S. Well, I don't know about that. The public library has noted itself as being "the poor man's college," the place for him or her to become educated, and it has succeeded admirably. I think there are very important people you can find who have gotten their education in that manner.

V.C. I couldn't agree with you more.

A.S. And since you knew what you wanted to get, you probably were definitely more oriented to learning than some people are when they go to college because they are not certain what they are going to be taking. This is reflected in your books, I think.

B.C. Vera started to write at a very early age. When she was nine, she would write different papers in her school room and sell them for twenty-five cents to the other students.

V.C. I wasn't greedy; I just needed the money.

A.S. Do you tell your audiences and young people when you talk to them these kinds of things?

V.C. Sure. But I don't think we should teach them how to write a book report by practically drawing them a blueprint. I don't think parents would approve of that. Times have changed; children don't need to do that anymore. Their parents give them the money.

B.C. We don't want to leave the impression that just because we quit school at an early age—neither of us finished high school—that others can quit school and become writers. It took us thirty years on that track to finally say we are writers.

A.S. We are attempting to show people today that there are equivalent routes to attain different things. A formal education isn't necessarily *the* only route. What I am trying to say is that they have to be motivated just as you were, and this shows in your works.

V.C. So many children ask us how we became writers; we get on an average of thirty to forty letters a week from readers. They ask, "How did you become a writer?" It is *my* contention that a writer is not made; the writer is born. As I said earlier in this interview, the writer views the world as his problem, and for some reason he wants to solve all these problems. He is terrified that he might die before he gets them all solved. Of course, he can't write about everything, so he has to select what interests him most. I cannot go along with the idea that there are certain facets of writing that may be taught. I think the writer is truly born with this curse, this illness, this gift, or whatever it is.

A.S. This wonderful, exciting, terrifying gift.

V.C. Yes, sometimes, it is.

A.S. Do you answer the children's letters?

V.C. Always.

B.C. Every one. We get several hundred letters a year and we personally answer each one.

V.C. We are getting beset more now by whole classes who write to us.

B.C. Yes. Each kid will have a question and sends it to the editor; then the editor mails the questions down to us.

V.C. We always answer letters from readers. I know there are some writers who do not; they say it takes too much time. Sure enough, it does take time; I haven't had a day off since the third of October. All day Sunday is spent making replies to these letters. When children write to a writer, they want an answer, and they don't want the answer six months hence; they want it now.

A.S. That's wonderful. You live up to the kinds of things you say in your stories.

JULIA CUNNINGHAM
Interviewed by M. Jerry Weiss

BOOKS BY JULIA CUNNINGHAM

Burnish Me Bright   Pantheon
Candle Tales   Pantheon
Dear Rat   (Avon)
Dorp Dead   Pantheon (Avon)
Far in the Day   Pantheon
Macaroon   Pantheon (Dell)
Maybe, A Mole   Pantheon (Dell)
Onion Journey   Pantheon
The Treasure is the Rose   Pantheon
Violett   Pantheon
The Vision of Francois the Fox   Pantheon

J.W. Hello. This is M. Jerry Weiss. I have the pleasure of interviewing Julia Cunningham, author of such books as *Burnish Me Bright* and *Come to the Edge*. Julia, how and when did you decide to become a writer?

J.C. I think, like a lot of people who become writers eventually, I started very young. I was about nine, I think. I found my first published story in an old trunk I have full of unpublished manuscripts. I like that old trunk. I never look at them anymore, but it's sort of like one's ashes—you ought to keep them.

J.W. Where did you get the idea for *Dorp Dead?*

J.C. I've been asked that a lot; I don't honestly know that I can answer it. I think that *Dorp Dead* started with the main character, Gilly. He sort of appeared to me in a curious kind of way, in that book, more than any other. Gilly stayed by my side while I was writing and sometimes I almost felt his presence. It was a very strange experience; I've never had it again with a character, though they're all very close to me.

J.W. Do you plan your book from beginning to end when you start writing? Do you have an outline?

J.C. Yes, I do have an outline. I know that a lot of beginning writers or would-be writers think an outline is tiresome, but it does help you to get over that terrible middle hump. You'll find sometimes you'll never finish a manuscript because you get to the middle and you don't know where to go from there, and your energy's giving out. That's why I have an outline, a very precise one, for the whole book. I don't always follow it; sometimes your characters lead you away from the plot and they contribute to the plot but, usually, I follow my own outline.

J.W. Have you a favorite character that you've created?

J.C. I think one of my favorites was the young French boy who was mute in *Burnish Me Bright.* I felt very close to him, too. I lived in France, luckily, for a year off and on, and it changed my whole feeling about language. I found in learning a new language that words in English became very precious to me because I couldn't speak their language. I was with people who didn't know any English at all, so I was forced to appreciate not only French, which I did, but also my own language became very real, almost as though it were illuminated. That's when I wrote the first book that was published. I had written many before, but I think I improved as a writer from the experience.

J.W. Did you have difficulty in getting your first book published?

J.C. Yes. I spent many years; in fact, I finally gave myself twelve years more and I was on the eleventh year when I thought, "Well, I'll try it once more." The letter came saying, "We're interested in meeting you; we think we're going to take your book." (This is Houghton-Mifflin.) When I got there, I asked the editor why she was interested in meeting me; she hadn't said "yes" and she hadn't said "no." She answered that they didn't know what age I was—whether I was eighteen or eighty. "If you were eighty," she said, "we couldn't have taken you on because you wouldn't have had a future." Since I wasn't eighty, they decided to give me a break.

J.W. Since that time, have you had any difficulty in getting any of your books published?

J.C. Yes. And I believe that writers shouldn't mind this. I have a very wonderful editor now at Pantheon books and he has turned down several of my manuscripts that I've written in the past years. He's such a good judge and such an honest person that I take his word for it and put those things away. That shouldn't discourage anybody who writes because, very often, you'll find when you put a manuscript away that that character will come up again in your life. It won't be the same person but it will be so like that person it's almost as though it were haunting you into a better book; so you generally end up writing a better book. You're not sorry. It's not easy to be turned down, ever. That's the one thing that discourages a lot of beginners, and if I have any advice, I would certainly say to keep on trying and keep on sending things out. One of my things was rejected twenty-seven times and that's a little too much; but it was finally published (that was *Dear Rat*). If you keep getting rejections, keep on sending out. Just try to think of them as sandwiches. Whatever you have, just send them all out in one day. They won't all come back in one day. Keep your hopes up. It's very hurtful, but it's a good thing to do.

J.W. Did they give you any reason as to why they rejected your book?

J.C. *Dear Rat* was turned down for a long, long time. They finally said they'd take a chance on it because it was about a rat. At that time, the only rat that was acceptable was the one in *The Wind in the Willows*, and that had become a classic. But they were very frightened about a book about a rat. They wouldn't be today, I don't think.

J.W. No. More and more books seem to be coming out, about all kinds of rats.

J.C. Yes—people rats.

J.W. Your characters seem to be so full of feelings and emotions. Is this intentional?

J.C. No. I think it just comes out of one's subconscious really; I think all of us have themes that we keep doing in some way, over and over, I suppose. People are interested in the fact that I always write about orphans, almost without exception. Naturally, the next question is, "Were you an orphan?" Actually, I wasn't. I had a very good childhood, in many ways. We've all had rotten ones, in other ways; orphans, for the purpose of the story, are very good people to write about because everything is against them. Of course, some people are orphaned in emotional, not physical, ways too. But they intrigue me. When I see a young person and suddenly there's that lovely contact and you are friends immediately, there's something orphaned about that person

Julia Cunningham

when I get to know him. We have a contact there, somewhere. That's a little hard to explain. We become friends.

J.W. The patron saint of the underdog.

J.C. That could be, Jerry, yes. I feel very strongly about that. I think we've all had that experience.

J.W. In your own reading experiences, were you influenced by people who created similar characters or similar situations or ideas of the underdog winning out in the end? Or are there any particular writers who seem to have left their mark on you?

J.C. No. I think we're all influenced by the writers we most like, but I can't really track that down. I can answer that a little obliquely in that I think the writer who has influenced my wishing to be a better writer is Georges Simenon who writes the Maigret mysteries and also writes very fine novels (well, they're all novels). I admire what he can say in three sentences where somebody else would take five pages. I recommend him to anyone who likes to read. He's easy to read, and you get this terrific feeling of people in his books. All the libraries have them, hopefully.

J.W. What advice would you have for someone who would like to be a writer?

J.C. I think you have to do it, first of all, because you want to, and there are so many reasons for wanting to. When I talk to people younger than myself, very often loneliness or misfortunes of some kind will spur someone to become a writer. You find another country for yourself; it's a place you can go and have adventures there. I think if a beginning writer feels this excitement and joins in with the characters, you sort of let yourself go and have fun with it, basically. There's a lot of talk about the pain and agony of writing, and it certainly isn't an easy thing to do; but when you're beginning, simply sit down with a pen or a typewriter, or whatever you're familiar with, and just let it ride, just like a stream of consciousness almost, and let it go; don't bother about punctuation or even grammar or anything else—you can do that later. Spelling's very unimportant at that point. Just write what comes from your emotions. You know, you worry about style but, gradually, you evolve your own style. But you must keep doing it. Like, you can't play the violin in a week. It's one of those things. You shouldn't worry about it; just do it as much as you can and as often as you care to. Another thing—keep it to yourself. There is the mistake a lot of parents make. I think they sometimes let people think their children are geniuses when they are not. And they expect too much from them. This will kill a beginning writer. Or a teacher will make too much of it, or maybe not enough, and there's hurt involved. Just keep it to yourself, and do it as your project, your very special, private thing.

J.W.   Do you find that writing is difficult for you?

J.C.   It isn't really, to me, no. I have a good habit about writing—and this helps if you're in difficulties—a lot of my writer friends sit in front of the typewriter for maybe half an hour, and they just wait and hope something is going to come out of it. That doesn't happen to me. I think that's partly because I have a very limited amount of time when I'm writing a book during the day, because I work the rest of the day. I get up early and write for just an hour. But it's always the same time (it could be six, seven, eight o'clock—whatever), and if you go at that very same hour every day, your insides will help you; you'll start. It's the time you started the day before and the past two weeks, and you're ready for it. That really is helpful, instead of just waiting for inspiration, or waiting until you're in a park, or something.

J.W.   Inspiration doesn't come on with a knight in shining armor.

J.C.   No, no. I think there's too much said about inspiration. That's inside you, but you don't have to worry about it—just let it happen. You're not always inspired, that's for sure. You can have lots of dull days; but write through those, too.

J.W.   Have you had many responses from readers of your books that have influenced your ideas or made you think about other kinds of books you would like to write?

J.C.   I've had lots of letters—as we all have—and I think the letters that I like the most are from older readers (I don't know anyone who likes to be called a "young adult") of *Dorp Dead.* So many of those letters have said, "You must have known Gilly, because I'm just like him." This surprises me, and I'm grateful for anybody writing this, because I had no idea that he would be like anybody. I get many of these letters, from boys especially, who will sit in the classroom and say, "I'm really very bright, but I don't want anyone to know it; it's none of their business." That's the way Gilly was. They do confide in you in letters, and it's a great honor. In that way, I guess I've been influenced, but I'm just sort of grateful. I think most of each book I write seems to come from a different area. Sometimes people say I haven't any pattern, but I don't really want one and I never tried to find one.

J.W. I'd say each book is different. You seem to have so many interesting experiences to share. I would imagine this would be quite difficult for most people because you draw on so many different kinds of areas of experience to hold your audiences. Where did you get the idea for *Come to the Edge*?

J.C. That started in a very small way. It was like seeing a flea or something. I heard the playwright Tom Stoppard talk, and he ended up his little lecture with a poem by an English poet about "Come to the Edge." In other words, we all come to the edge; don't be afraid of falling because you'll probably fly. I thought, "My, what a beautiful sentiment that is!" Instead of thinking you're going to go over the cliff, believe that you're going to sprout wings and fly. I could still get very thrilled over that. That's how that book got started. What I'd like to comment on, if I might, on *Burnish Me Bright* is that—this came to me after I wrote the book—I was mute, too, when I was unable to speak the language in France. I was really, really mute for at least four weeks, because I was shy as well; but I was learning as fast as I could. I felt the pain of muteness very, very sharply. You feel stupid and you feel unloved; nobody can understand you because you can't talk. I think that got into my being. That's why I loved Auguste so much—he had that problem, but he found a way out with pantomime. He was lucky he found somebody who helped him.

J.W. Do you think because of the endings of your books you're more romantic than real?

J.C. I've been called a romanticist, just because I have happy endings. I kind of believe in happy endings. Life doesn't have a lot of happy endings, but I think books should; and I think that's part of the art of fiction, frankly. That sounds awfully intellectual, but I do think fiction should come to a roundness of some kind. I don't mind an open end, but it shouldn't be so open that the person has committed suicide. I've had arguments with writers (whose names I won't mention—I respect them very much) who do end their books this way. I think that's a pity because the reader does have to have some sort of satisfaction, I think. It doesn't have to be entirely happy, but there's got to be a little tiny bit of light at the end of the tunnel. In my books it's a matter of faith with me; I must do that.

J.W. I think this is important, too, because so many students, so many young adults do want to find answers to ways of coping, and they want to know, even with the problems they face, that there is some hope of a way of resolving conflict. You seem to be able to give us that kind of hope through your books.

J.C.   Thank you. I hope it's there.

J.W.   Gilly certainly is a marvelous example, and I must admit he fascinates me. Have you had any letters from adults about *Dorp Dead?*

J.C.   Yes, I've had lots; from teachers, mainly. They want to know about the symbolism in the book. I suppose it is full of symbols, but I wasn't thinking about them. I was just thinking about them as people. The "Hunter" who is never named—I get letters from young people about that and I don't mind being honest with them about that. I never did know what the man's name was. A teacher will write and say, "Was he Jesus Christ?" I'm not criticizing this now but, of course, he wasn't Jesus Christ; he was the hunter, whatever his name was. He chose to remain anonymous except to the boy, and I didn't know why the readers should know; I wasn't let in on it, either. This symbol-seeking is, I think, a mistake. I think it must spoil the books for many people; the analyzing of it. I've never heard any of it, but I've read. Then you get letters from college students who are doing papers, for instance, on your books, and they want to know the reasons for this and the reasons for that. There really aren't any. It's like writing; if you've done it long enough, it is as natural as breathing, in a curious way. It's work, but it's also breathing, and you can't really explain why you breathe or why you want to.

J.W.   Maybe this is from a society that has been taught to analyze, perchance, too much. Things happen in a certain way; we ought to let them happen and not try to be so critical and analytical. I think that many, many students feel that reading can be so analytical that the enjoyment is taken away.

J.C.   It's sort of squeezed out, I think, in many cases; that, and abridgement and all those other things that happen to books. I've been lucky, though; I'll probably never be a wild success and I don't mind that. I don't think success has much to do with the whole profession. You do the best you can—that may sound like a cliche—but you do the best you can at that moment and just hope that it will turn out to be a good book. Sometimes it does; sometimes it doesn't.

J.W.   What is a successful writer, in your opinion?

J.C.   I think in the world's view—and fifth and sixth graders never fail to ask the question—"How much money do you make?" We don't mind this question at all; we all get it, and we just explain about percentages and things. They never find out how much we make or don't make. I think, though, in the world's view, it's what your royalties amount to, or how much publicity you get, or whatever. I don't know; I haven't much vanity and I'm lucky that way and it isn't a virtue because I was so long in being published, it wore me out. Maybe if I'd been published at twenty-two, I'd be sort of puffed-up about it all. But I passed through all that, I think.

J.W.   I understand that one of your books has been optioned, possibly, for a movie?

J.C.   Yes. This happened to both *Burnish Me Bright* and *Dorp Dead;* and, of course, movies are pretty chancy, so that never happened. But this latest option is they may make an animated cartoon feature out of *Dear Rat*, which I think would be loads of fun. I wouldn't have anything to do with it; it would be in the hands of the moviemaker.

J.W.   Does this concern you—that you won't have any opportunity to have input or control over the finished product you created that's transferred to another medium?

J.C.   I don't really think so, Jerry, because it is another medium and it's a medium I can't handle. I couldn't any more write a screenplay than I could build a table.

J.W.   We talked to an author not too long ago who wrote a marvelous story about the South and he was asked to serve as a consultant. Sure enough, when Hollywood got hold of his story, they were going to make a western out of it. This is what I meant by control or input or making sure that the characters still remain faithful to the book as you created them. Does this bother you?

J.C.   No. I think when you agree to sell a property like that, you have to be satisfied to stay away from it, unless you are a screenwriter and know the movie business. When they got together a company to make *Dorp Dead*, it came very, very close; they even knew where they were going to film it—in Yugoslavia, I believe—and had the town and everything all set. Then things fell through at the last minute. I met the crew and they thought I was going to make a little bit of trouble for them, a little flack, because they were changing the plot. They had to change the plot to some extent, to make a film out of it. Much of this book is literary, they said; it's the reading that's powerful. Go ahead, I said and they sort of cheered. The crew really ended up liking me very much. They said, "We'd like you to come to Yugoslavia; we weren't going to ask you, but we'd like you to come," which I thought was a compliment. But we never did go.

J.W. Do you think it might possibly be picked up again?

J.C. I don't know; I've had three or four options on that. Somebody may make it sometime. Really, it wouldn't make a bad movie.

J.W. Have you ever seen a movie based on someone else's book that you've read and, as an author, felt for the writer?

J.C. Yes, I've felt very sorry sometimes. That's certainly true in the adult field. They do twist books around. Once in a while, they do make a good one, but I think in the children's book field, things I've seen like (I don't know if I should mention names) *Charlotte's Web* and some of those things and *Willy Wonka* from *Charlie and The Chocolate Factory* were really dreadful, dreadful films and it's a pity because they had such good material available. *Willy Wonka* didn't have to be that bad. I think the sets pretty much killed it for me; they were very cheap looking.

J.W. What do you think the difference is in seeing a movie or watching a television program as compared to reading a book?

J.C. I'll tell you the truth—I've liked movies ever since I was first taken to one. I'm a movie buff; I'm fascinated with them and I enjoy very much going to them. I also love horror films; I'm quite an expert on those. I worked for a movie magazine for five years for Dell and I enjoyed that. I used to go into their files on my lunch hours and read things and look at pictures and things; I love movies. But I also love to read; I don't know—I like any kind of entertainment, actually. I love to go to school plays. I like doing all that.

J.W. Let me ask you one final question, if I may. You've chosen children's and young adult literature for the most part, on which to concentrate your efforts as a writer. Is there a reason you've chosen those areas as compared with choosing adult fiction or nonfiction as an area of specialization? Does it bother you that you have not written the adult novel?

J.C. No. Sometimes people do, in a very polite way, criticize us and say, "Someday, you'll write an adult novel." We all sort of chuckle because in a lot of ways the shorter book is harder to accomplish well. I didn't actually choose. I think maybe I'm trying to go back, without realizing it, to a part of my own life that I'm trying to resolve and I think this may be true of many, many writers. We can't pinpoint it, but there are things I've felt strongly about and they just come out in books and they just happen to be published as "young adult" or "children's" books. I like the forms.

J.W. What are some of these things you feel so strongly about that should be in books for young adults?

J.C. One of the things we discussed before—a way out. I think that everybody needs it. I feel very humble about this. If I've contributed in any way, I'm very grateful to hear it. I like to see a life somewhat resolved.

J.W. I think these are the most honorable characteristics of your books. I think that students and young readers (and I) find sincerity and honesty and beauty and suspense in your stories. You create this and make us want to become a Julia Cunningham reader forevermore. Please keep at it. And, thank you very much.

J.C. Thank you, Jerry.

S. E. HINTON

Interviewed by William Walsh

BOOKS BY S. E. HINTON

The Outsiders   (Dell)
Rumblefish   (Dell)
That Was Then, This Is Now   (Dell)

W.W.   How does a sixteen-year-old come to write a novel that is such a best seller and such a popular novel?

S.E.H.   I've been practicing writing for eight years. I started in grade school, and I had written a couple of other novels before *The Outsiders*. It was just the first I ever tried to publish.

W.W.   Tell us the story of why you sent this one out, when you hadn't sent any others.

S.E.H.   The mother of a girlfriend of mine writes children's books, and she read *The Outsiders* and liked it. She said she would give me the name of her agency and told me to send it to them to see what they could do with it. Finally, I thought it would be worth a try, and I did send it.

W.W.   Did this inspire you to burn the midnight oil?

S.E.H.   Oh, no. It inspired me so greatly that I was unable to write for four years. I had a super case of "first novel block." I could not write for four years. I could not use the typewriter, even to write a letter, even though I taught myself to type when I was in the sixth grade. I love to write, but for four years, I could not. I was a teenage writer, which is very similar to being a teenage werewolf. People are always watching you for signs of "things." I was put in the spotlight. I can understand

S.E. Hinton

complications people have who are suddenly famous overnight. Even though the amount of fame I got was very small, compared to that of a lot of people at the same age, it was enough to really bother me.

W.W. Where did you get the material to write the story, *The Outsiders?*

S.E.H. Well, it dealt with a situation I had in high school: The Socialist-Greasers thing, which is a very small part, because I went to a large high school and everybody was divided up into different camps. The Socialists and the Greasers were actually just the extremes. There were all kinds of middle groups like the "artsy-craftsy" people; the "student council" people; "greasy socialists," and "socialist-greasers." It was a complicated social situation. I thought it was a very dumb situation, on top of that.

W.W. Did you belong to one of these groups yourself?

S.E.H. No. Even the nonconformists would not have me, because I wouldn't conform. But I had friends from all different groups. I thought it was dumb; but nobody questioned it.

W.W. You were accepted, though, by people in all the different groups?

S.E.H. Yes, Well, everyone looked at me sort of strangely, but I was accepted. I was a pretty good fighter; I did not scream when the police chased us; and I had a pretty good-sized switchblade knife that everybody liked. I was treated as one of the guys. I got my tooth chipped when I was hit in the face with a bottle. I had an interesting adolescence.

W.W. There's a crucial scene in the book where Johnnycake is dying in the hospital. He sees PonyBoy and he says, "Stay gold, PonyBoy; stay gold." Now, we remember, earlier on, that they were taught Robert Frost's poem, "Nothing Gold Can Stay." Did you have anything else in mind beyond that?

S.E.H. Not really. While I was writing the book, I had no idea of plot structure—I still don't, I can't plot my way out of the Safe-Way Store—but I know my characters. And, during the book, I would go so far as to say to my friends, "I'm writing a book; this is what's happened so far. What should happen next?" And they would tell me something, and I'd stick it in. The fire scene was something somebody told me ("Hey! Make the church catch on fire!" "Okay, I'll do that."). But, as far as the poem goes, I was working on my book in a creative writing class (which I made a "D" in because I was writing my book and not doing my class work), and I read the Robert Frost poem. I enjoyed it, and thought it was appropriate for my book and I stuck it in. I liked the feeling of it, the enthusiasm and the innocence and everything you lose as you get older. You lose your emotional commitments and I think that's what Frost had in mind. That's what I had in mind, even though I probably could not have articulated it at that time.

W.W.   Was there a PonyBoy Curtis? I mean, I know you say there was a general situation, but . . . .

S.E.H.   Not really. I couldn't point out any kid that I knew as a child and say that that was PonyBoy; but he was very much like I was at that age. Maybe a lot of things happened to him that happened to different friends of mine. Not all of his experiences were one person's experiences. I just incorporated them. I've learned as a writer that any character you write is going to turn out to be some aspect of yourself, so there's an awful lot of me in Dallas Winston as well as PonyBoy Curtis. I don't think as a writer you can really, truthfully, say this person is so-and-so; it has to be filtered through your mind, so it is some part of you.

W.W.   You said before that you couldn't plot your way out of Safe-Way and that, very often, others suggested elements of plot that you would put into the novel. Were the characters the same way? Do you have a clear idea of the character?

S.E.H.   I have an absolutely clear conception of my characters. If they walked through the door, I wouldn't be surprised. I know their birthdays, what they like to eat for breakfast; I know what kind of dreams they have; I know their hair color, their eye color. One thing I cannot stand. It happened when I was reading one of Harold Robbins' books. I got halfway through the book, and he switched his character's eye color on me, and I just shut the book. I thought, "If the man doesn't know his character well enough to know what color his eyes are, I don't really care to read his work." I'm a very strong character writer, but that is only myself. There are other writers, like Ray Bradbury, who are idea writers; there are people who are atmosphere writers; people who can do intricate plots. Everybody has his own strong point. Mine is character.

W.W.   When you wrote *That Was Then*, did it also come out of some personal experience?

S.E.H.   It's hard to say because you mix up things that have happened to other people with your own experiences, and you take what your own experiences might have been and dramatize them into something completely different. You get your characters from different places.

Like Mark, one of the main characters in *That Was Then*. His personality was taken directly from a cat I had (people think this is a cute, funny, little writer-thing you say). I actually got his personality from a cat, as much as I can get a personality from a human being. Later, I was talking to my sister (who is also a cat-person) and told her I had gotten Mark from Rabbit—my cat—and she said, "Oh, yes. I see that." Rabbit had beautiful beer-colored eyes that I had to incorporate into the character. And he's a completely amoral little animal. What was good for him was good; what was bad for him was bad. He had no judgments, so far as how his actions might affect other people.

W.W.   This mixing up your life with other people's and then sorting it out in a book, does that help you understand yourself or your experiences better?

S.E.H.   Sometimes. But it takes several years to look back on it and see what you were actually saying; I feel like the theme in *That Was Then* was "growth is betrayal" and, even though I knew that was what I wanted to say, when I got through with it, I was satisfied that I had it said. I still could not put it into words until four or five years later.

W.W.   You said it better than you knew. I think many writers have that experience. A lot of what you're doing is unconscious or subconscious.

S.E.H.   It is completely subconscious; and later you can look back and say, "I did this," or "I did that." Like in *Rumblefish,* I had somebody remark upon the color symbolism I used (black and white motif) and I didn't realize that I had done it until I looked back and saw; not only with the color blindness of the motorcycle boy, but the different things of black and white and black and white and black and white that go out through the story.

W.W.   Speaking about *Rumblefish*, at one point Rusty James becomes color blind. Is there a set parallel we're supposed to see?

S.E.H.   There's supposed to be, even more so, at the end of the book when he's talking to Steve and he starts listening to the ocean; he doesn't hear Steve. And the motorcycle boy was notoriously bad on his hearing. I thought it would be interesting to show two completely different people, one very complex, one very simple, who went through the same battering set of circumstances and came out relatively the same at the end, even though the cause and the effect worked on completely different things. This kind of numbness—Rusty James didn't care if he saw Steven, didn't care about anything; he liked sitting there looking at the ocean all day—was somewhat the same regarding the motorcycle boy's detachment that he would just see things and not get involved with anything. He didn't belong anywhere. I enjoyed doing that book because I felt it was a challenge to me as a writer. It would have been very easy for me to write a sequel to *The Outsiders* or a sequel to *That Was Then* and go into *The Curtis Boys Visit the Farm* and that sort of thing, but I wanted to do something different and Rusty James is different. He's not articulate, observant, or intelligent. It is difficult to write a book from his point of view. As a writer, I was very happy with the book.

W.W. That's an interesting thing you said. The feeling you get from reading *Rumblefish* is quite different from the feeling you get from *The Outsiders* and also from *That Was Then*. They are all first-person narrations, and it seems that it is the narrator who is changing in each case, and the world appears different, as each person sees it.

S.E.H. I try to do that. I could take PonyBoy Curtis and change his name to "Jim Smith" or something and write another book from the same person's point of view; but that's not stretching yourself as a writer, and I want to do that. At the same time, I still want to reach my own audience. I write for kids who don't usually read a book, so I feel that *Rumblefish* is written on two different levels, when it's one. Just a simple, straight story, a little action thing, how Rusty James couldn't let go of the good old days of the gangs, and how that destroyed him. But I still feel, at least from the letters I've gotten from kids, they realize there's something else there, even if they don't know what it is. They think, "I've got to think about that. Maybe I don't know what it means, but it's something to think about and maybe I'll come back to it later." I think I accomplished what I set out to do with *Rumblefish*.

W.W. Do any of the youngsters who write to you ask you about their own writing?

S.E.H. Yes, they do. A lot of them want to write and don't know where to begin. I always say that, first of all, they've got to read. Just read everything. I never studied writing consciously. But if you read a lot, like I did, subconsciously, structure is going to drop into your head, whether it's sentence structure, paragraph structure, chapter structure, or novel structure. Pretty soon, you're going to know where things go— where the climax is supposed to be, where the ending's supposed to be, how to get there, how to describe people. You can absorb it subconsciously. I, personally, never tried to copy any one person's style because I feel you should write the way you think. But reading lots of different styles will expose you to different ways of thinking. My big recommendation is to read and then practice. Write yourself. I wrote for eight years before I wrote *The Outsiders*. I advise writing for oneself. If you don't want to read it, nobody else is going to read it. Once you do that and get somebody else's opinion, just start sending it away.

W.W. Who's your favorite character—of your own? Or your favorite book?

S.E.H. That's hard to say because *The Outsiders* sort of made my fame, but I see so many things wrong with it as a writer that I can't say that's the best writing I've ever done. Another thing, it's been very hard for me to accept the fact that it's very likely that the first book I've ever written will be the book I'll be known for ("Oh, you're the person who wrote *The Outsiders*"). As far as characters go, although Mark is not a particularly admirable character, I feel he's a very vivid character in *That Was Then*; and that silly motorcycle boy who just drove me nuts— would not leave me be—I saw his picture in *Life Magazine* just as I described it in the book when Rusty James is going into the drugstore and he's reading a magazine. I had to write that book and describe the motorcycle boy; I probably still do not do him justice. It's hard, like when you ask someone, "Which is your favorite child?"

W.W. Do you have any new children in the typewriter?

S.E.H. I'm working on a book now, but I really don't like to talk about it, except that I'm very happy with the main character.

W.W. All of your character-narrators are first person, male.

S.E.H. I can't write from a female point of view. I've tried it, but I can't do it. It's just that when I was growing up, all my close friends were guys. I identified with the male culture; I was a tomboy; and, while I realize now I used to think I had a male mind, I think I just had a female mind that didn't conform to the female culture at that time. It's just a thing I feel very comfortable with, and I realize I reach all my audience that way. While girls will read boys' books, boys very often will not read girls' books; so one can appeal to both of them that way. It's very likely I will continue to write from the male point of view.

W.W. You don't think there's a great deal of difference, then, between the point of view of a fifteen year-old boy and a fifteen year-old girl?

S.E.H. Not as much as you would think, really. It's amazing the similarities among the letters I get from guys and girls. If they could just

Interviewed by William Walsh   37

realize that this artificial barrier between them is almost just socially set up, that their wishes, their dreams and everything are very similar, they could communicate a lot better.

S.E. Hinton

ISABELLE HOLLAND

Interviewed by Paul Janeczko

BOOKS BY ISABELLE HOLLAND

Alan and the Animal Kingdom   Lippincott
Amanda's Choice   Lippincott
Cecily   Lippincott
Darcourt   Fawcett World
The De Maury Papers   Rawson Associates
Grenelle   Fawcett World
Heads You Win, Tails I Lose   Lippincott (Dell)
Hitchhike   Lippincott
The Man without a Face   Lippincott (Bantam)
Moncrifee   Fawcett World
Of Love and Death and other Journeys   Lippincott
    (Dell)
Tower Abbey   Rawson Associates
Trelawny   (Bantam)

P.J.   How did you get started writing?

I.H.   I think I started writing because my mother was a storyteller, and I basically think of myself as a storyteller. I write story-type novels, whether it's young adult, or children's, or adult novels. I grew up in non-English speaking countries until the age of seven, which meant I was very much with my family. My earliest memories are of being told a great number of stories, and I think the distance from listening to storytelling is fairly short. I did publish my first story at about the age of twelve.

P.J.   Where do you get the ideas for your books?

I.H.   I think I usually start off with the idea of a relationship or an enmity, which becomes a relationship between two people—frequently between a young person and an adult, because I am more interested in that than I am in relationships between adults and children. Everything else that comes into the story after that is added. The relationship starts off with enmity or hostility and becomes something else, and that is the basic theme that interests me.

P.J.   How long does it take you to write a book?

I.H.   Anywhere from two months to six months, although my first book, *Cecily*, took six years.

P.J.   How about some of your more recent ones?

I.H.   *The Man without a Face* took four months; *Of Love and Death and other Journeys* took about the same time. I have two new books: *Alan and the Animal Kingdom*, which is for ages eight to twelve, is already published and only took me about two months to write. The other book is *Hitchhike*, and it took me the same length of time.

P.J.   What is your writing routine?

I.H.   I try to write fairly soon after I get up in the morning for a minimum of three hours. Sometimes I go to four. It doesn't always work out that way; I have business things I have to do and sometimes trips, which interrupt, but the earlier in the day I write, the better it is.

P.J.   Do you do a lot of rewriting?

I.H.   No. Each day I usually try to aim for between four and six or seven pages. When I sit down to work in the morning I read over the pages I did the day before, and I make changes then. It is very rare that I make them much beyond that except for a general sort of light editing when I read it through at the end.

P.J.   Do you write from your own experiences?

I.H.   I write from my own experiences in the sense that the things that I write about, which are often isolation or an inability to have a good relationship or the acceptance of a problem, have been my own. But the plots themselves are not necessarily out of my own experiences because I have frequently written in the first person from the point of view of boys; but I think that what they feel is the same as what I have felt.

P.J.   In your opinion, what is the essence of good writing?

I.H.   The essence of good writing is the ability to portray people with

Isabelle Holland

absolute conviction, and to do it with a certain craftsmanship of language.

P.J. Is that something that a person can learn?

I.H. I think that the use of language is certainly something a person can learn. I am not sure whether storytelling is a learned thing. Many good writers are not particularly good storytellers. That's a different category. I think that a good teacher can take somebody who wants to be a writer and, through instruction and editing, show him how to write with truth rather than with sentimentality.

P.J. Is theme a conscious effort or do you merely try to tell a good story and let the theme surface within that story?

I.H. I try to tell a good story and let the theme surface, because I think the moment you tell a story to make a point of something, then you are manipulating it; and, by extension, you are trying to manipulate the reader.

P.J. Of the books you've written, which is your favorite?

I.H. I suppose *The Man without a Face* is still my favorite.

P.J. What do you feel you owe your readers?

I.H. Only an honest job. I don't feel I owe them anything except a story as well told as I can tell it, anymore than they owe it to me to read it. It's sort of a mutual pleasure-pact on our part; if they like what they read enough to look for another of my books, then that's not an obligation they have to me. That is something they do for themselves and, basically, writing is something I do for myself. If the readers and I come together in this, then I think it's a mutually beneficial arrangement.

P.J. Do you do other writing besides your books for young people?

I.H. Yes. I write what are called novels of Gothic suspense for adults, although I think that teenagers also enjoy them, especially girl teenagers. They are also basically story novels.

P.J. Was there a specific person who influenced you or inspired you to become a writer?

I.H. Probably my mother, in the sense that she was such a tremendously good storyteller herself that I think this shaped me at a very early age. I also had one or two good teachers who helped me. I think that kind of help comes early or it doesn't come at all.

P.J. What would you do if you were not a writer?

I.H.   Although I don't have any talent, if I could have my pick, if I were not a writer, I would like to play in a string ensemble.

P.J.   You play the piano?

I.H.   Very poorly, and lately I have taken up the recorder. The piano is a very solitary instrument and you need to be particularly good. I cannot play well enough to be pleased with it. So I went to the New School and took a beginner's course in the recorder. I play with a class, and I play very badly—I can't get either the top or bottom notes—but I get a lot of pleasure out of playing with the group.

P.J.   What advice would you give young people who want to become writers?

I.H.   More than anything else, to keep on writing. I think—I cannot stress this enough—that the habit of writing is the most important thing a writer can develop. And, to write every day, even a small amount, I think is much more important than writing a lot occasionally.

P.J.   Were you a reader as a young adult?

I.H.   Yes. I was not a particularly advanced reader, but I read when I was a young adult, everything from schoolgirl stories (which were very fashionable in the England in which I was brought up), all the way up to George Eliot, Jane Austen, Dickens, etc. I was a very catholic reader; I read everything that came my way, not particularly intellectual about it, not particularly advanced, but I remember the time I got hold of *Gone With the Wind*—I think I was seventeen years old—and I swallowed that whole.

P.J.   In an age of creative writing, how important is grammar?

I.H.   I think it's very, very important. It's like saying, "How important is structure to building a house?" I think you have to learn the rules before you can break them. And I think that language is one of the most beautiful arts that there is in the world—any language. To learn how to use it, its strength and its suppleness, you can only learn the hard way, by learning grammar. I think once you've learned it, you can then learn how to break the rules. When I watch a dancer like Nureyev, or a violinist, I realize that hours of very dreary practice went into that, even though the performance looks absolutely effortless by the time I watch or listen. There is no substitute for hard work in the early years.

P.J.   Is writing hard work?

Isabelle Holland

I.H.   Very hard work. It's also a great pleasure. There are times when it's more hard work than it is pleasure, just as there are times when it's more pleasure than it is hard work.

P.J.   Thank you.

MOLLIE HUNTER

Interviewed by Jean Greenlaw

BOOKS BY MOLLIE HUNTER

A Furl of Fairy Wind   Harper and Row
The Haunted Mountain   Harper and Row
The Kelpie's Pearls   Harper and Row
A Sound of Chariots   Harper and Row (Avon)
A Stranger Came Ashore   Harper and Row
The Stronghold   Harper and Row (Avon)
Talent Is Not Enough   Harper and Row
Thirteenth Member   Harper and Row
Walking Stones   Harper and Row
The Wicked One   Harper and Row

J.G.   I have the pleasure of interviewing Mollie Hunter. Mollie lives in Scotland, and is the author of many books published in the United States. She won the British Carnegie Medal for *The Stronghold* and has written other historical novels and fantasies. She has also written a book of essays on writing entitled *Talent is Not Enough*. Titles of her books include *The Stronghold, A Sound of Chariots, A Stranger Came Ashore*, and *The Haunted Mountain*. Mollie, would you tell us a bit about yourself, your home, and your family.

M.H.   My home is in a small mountain valley in the north of Scotland. We call that kind of a mountain valley a glen. It's a house that's built in a very traditional style, of stone. It has a lovely outlook, overlooking the mountains. I live there with my husband and two very large dogs which I have to exercise every day. I have two sons: one is a soldier and one practices osteopathy. He lives quite near me and he has three children so that I see my grandchildren quite often. My day is spent mostly in writing, but I get out a lot, mostly because of those dogs I have to exercise. My house is part of a village of about thirty houses, and the people there are my friends. We have a warm, very friendly sort of community life in the Highlands. They don't pay a great deal of attention to my being a writer; I'm just a person in the village. "Glen folk" we call ourselves. Altogether I think I live a very pleasant, comfortable life, although I work very hard, because writing is a hard job. I have to travel quite a bit, mostly in connection with my writing, but also sometimes just for the sheer fun of it. The thing I like best about travelling is coming home again.

J.G. Many of your books for young adults are historical fiction— *The Stronghold*, for example. Why do you choose this form, and where do you get your ideas?

M.H. I think I'll answer that last question first. It's one that I'm often asked, and I always find it a bit funny because, to me, it gives the impression that you can sort of go to the store and buy ideas; but it doesn't happen that way. If you're a writer, you just happen to have been born with a particular kind of mind. What happens, in effect, is that your mind is full of a series of little pictures without your realizing it, and your brain, of course, is the finest computer ever invented. If you're a writer, there is perhaps a little extra quality that you have which will make two of these pictures which don't have any connection, really, click into place, and you see that they connect in a way, and you have the beginning of a story. Suddenly, this computer which is your brain has clicked them together—really, you may have seen them years apart, or in totally different situations. That's where ideas come from. I choose historical fiction because I'm interested in the past, and it just so happens that the past is all around me in the circumstances in which I live; there are reminders of it, for instance, in the form of old buildings. And, I've always been curious about what happened before I was born, and I've done a lot of research to find out. But I also have the sense of all the people who lived before me and I like to try to recreate their lives because, to me, the people who lived in the past were no different; in fact, it's not just to me they were no different; they actually were no different from ourselves. And I just like the sensation of wandering back into the past. It's like a country that I have come to know. I like walking through the past and coming back into my own time with a good story to tell.

J.G. You've also written fantasies. What is the essential message you're trying to convey to your readers in your fantasies?

M.H. I think I would like to say, first of all, without wanting to seem as if I'm lecturing, that if you're trying to convey a message, as such, then you can't tell a good story. People don't like to be told; they don't like to feel that they have to do something. But I've got strong ideas about things and about people, and they're woven into the form of a story so that people are reading my ideas without realizing that these are ideas. As far as the fantasies are concerned, they always concern real people in real situations; but, at some point in the story, these people encounter something to do with the supernatural. Things happen as a result of that, and sometimes they can be very dangerous situations with the people in danger of being drawn into something very powerful, very evil. In these circumstances, there is nothing they can do except rely on the one thing humans have that supernatural beings don't have, and that is a soul. Because of that, human beings have the capacity to love. Now, if you attempt to practice magic against something, you must understand it. And, if any supernatural being tries to bring the power of magic against love, it is helpless to do so because, if you have no soul, you cannot love; you cannot understand love and, therefore, you have no power against it. I think that, if there is a message, it is that the most powerful force on earth is the capacity of human beings to reach out, to be warm, responsive to one another—to love.

J.G. You have written, using many characters out of folklore. Do you create your own? Does this come out of lore you already know from your background?

M.H. Oh, yes. I've used many types of characters from folklore, perhaps some that my readers haven't heard of before, because folklore is so extensive; for instance, I don't think that before a young American reader has read *The Kelpie's Pearls*, he will have heard of an *Urisk*, because that's a Gallic word. You'd only hear it in the Highlands of Scotland (but it's well known in the lower of the Highlands). I've used another character, too, *Bean Nighe*, another Gallic word. It means "the washer by the ford," another supernatural creature—very dangerous, very inimical to human beings. In my last book, however, I have invented a totally new character which is supernatural. I'm getting a bit fed up with stories that are so dead serious, and everyone is taking things so earnestly, that I made up my mind that I would have a bit of fun and a good laugh. Although it is so horrible that nobody can bear to look at it, I hope. I managed to project this creature into a story which is funny to read. It finished up in America, by the way, although it starts out in the Highlands.

Mollie Hunter

J.G. Your books are all excellent examples of beautiful command of language. How did you develop this appreciation of and the ability to use language so well?

M.H. I think that one is born with an appreciation of language, in the same way that you're born with a good ear for music, but the capacity to use language in my case was most certainly initiated by the way I was taught at school. I had, as a result of the circumstances I was in, to leave school when I was fourteen years old; but, by the time I had done so, I had grasped the language simply as a result of the fact that every English lesson consisted partly, at least, of a passage which had to be analyzed. I had to analyze sentences so that I understood what the structure of language was. Then we had to do a passage which we called precis. I don't know what you might call it here, but it was simply a long passage that had to be condensed, keeping the essential meaning of it. Now this meant that we were taught to understand the structure of language; we were taught to search for the words which had the strongest and most extensive meaning and to replace that whole sentence with that one word. I have found that when I have difficulty with a passage of any kind, I sit back and say to myself, "What do you really want to say?" And then I write it in the briefest way possible. I use the minimum of words to get the essential idea. I was trained to do this when I was very young and I have continued to use this kind of training.

J.G. So many of our students get impatient when they're asked to rewrite something. As an author, do you feel you have a need to rewrite?

M.H. Oh, yes. Some—in fact, most—of my manuscripts can only be read by myself; they have been rewritten so often. I write in longhand, using a ballpoint pen. I may start writing using a blue pen; then I'll go back over what I've done and I'll correct this in a black pen; then I'll go back over that and correct it in a red pen. I'll make corrections in the margin; I have asterisks and arrows which carry the eye over the page; I use quarter-size pages; yet, my manuscripts are very seldom changed for any reason whatsoever because the final typed manuscript is always immaculate. When my editors see the original manuscript, they are amazed because each side of these quarter pages is written and rewritten and written again. I can't think that there are writers so clever or naturally so good at this sort of thing that they can do anything without rewriting. There could be a genius in every generation, I suppose, but not very many.

J.G. You have a book of essays titled, *Talent is Not Enough*. What led you to write the book?

M.H. In 1975, I had to come to America to give the Arbuthnot Lecture and I wanted to keep a very strong, essential thread in this lecture. In order to do that, I could only touch very lightly, very passingly, on the aspects of my work that I would have liked to explore more deeply. So, when I finished writing the Arbuthnot lecture, because I had to give talks in various other places following Arbuthnot, I decided that I would explore these themes, these aspects of my work that I had set aside. I would explore them at greater length. I had reached the stage, I felt, where I wanted to be definitive about my craft, about what is involved in it—not just in terms of the background research that has been necessary for it, but the actual technique of my craft. I decided that this was the opportunity to do it. Not just for the benefit of the people who would hear it and get something out of it, but for my own benefit. I wanted to be very clear in my mind about certain things, and also there were things I had wanted for a long time to say. I have very strong ideas on certain subjects and I thought, this is the chance to say them; this is the time to really tell people what I think about these things. I wasn't sure whether anybody would want to hear them; but, as it turned out, people were interested, to the point where they wanted to read these lectures in book form. And the book was begun, therefore.

J.G. These books would be very interesting to someone who wanted to be a writer, but if you had just one piece of advice to an aspiring writer, what would it be?

M.H. Write every day, even if it's only your own name. Get into the habit of writing. It was an American—Thomas Edison—who said that genius is one-tenth inspiration, nine-tenths perspiration. When we started talking like this, I said that I enjoyed my life, which is mostly taken up by writing, but that writing is hard work. You have to have a disciplined approach to it, and the beginning of the discipline is to write every day. You get into the habit of writing; you get into the habit of the thinking patterns that are necessary; and you don't have to drive yourself to your desk ever after that. You're in the habit of going to your desk; and when you're in the habit of going to your desk to write, you become a writer.

J.G. Thank you, Mollie, an author whose talent and discipline have allowed you to create many fine books for us.

M. E. KERR

Interviewed by Paul Janeczko

BOOKS BY M. E. KERR

Dinky Hocker Shoots Smack   Harper and Row (Dell)
Gentlehands   Harper and Row (Bantam)
If I Love You Am I Trapped Forever?   Harper and
   Row (Dell)
I'll Love You When You're More Like Me   Harper and
   Row (Dell)
Is That You, Miss Blue   Harper and Row (Dell)
Love is a Missing Person   Harper and Row (Dell)
The Son of Someone Famous   Harper and Row
   (Ballantine)

M.E.K. Ever since I can remember, I wanted to be a writer. My
father's initials were E.R.M., and he had stationery with his initials on
it. When I was around eleven, I invented the pseudonym "Eric
Ranthram McKay" and began sending out stories signed with that
name. My letter to the editor was written on my Dad's stationery. I sent
stories to all the magazines and I received so many rejection slips that
one Halloween I went to a costume party as a rejection slip. I wore a slip
with all my rejection notices pinned to it. By the way, a rejection slip is a
small printed form that says, "Thank you very much for sending in your
work, but . . . . " I don't know what made me want to be a writer except
that I was always a watcher of other people. I'd sit on the stairs in our
house when I was very little, around four or five, and I would be
watching the neighbors through a Venetian blind slat. I liked to
overhear conversations, too. If my mother and dad had a party, I was
always at the top of the stairs listening, or on the extension when

someone in my family was using the telephone. I loved gossip, even when it was about people I didn't know. My mother was a great gossip, and I always felt a certain thrill of excitement as stories of the neighbors would unfold day by day like a soap opera. My dad had a very large library and I read every book in it, except the ones on mathematics and science. They were all poor subjects. I loved Dickens and Dostoevsky and Emerson's essays and all poetry. But my tastes weren't above stories in magazines like *Good Housekeeping*, any newspaper stories, gossip columns, and popular novels—things we'd call best seller material today, the kinds of books Jacqueline Susann wrote and Harold Robbins writes. I guess I liked to read anything, and I always thought some day I'd be a writer and write about the kids I went to school with, my family, my friends' families. I chose to go to the University of Missouri, although I was from New York State, because I heard there was a fantastic Journalism School at Missouri. I didn't think I'd ever earn my living as a writer of stories; that seemed like an impossible dream, so I thought the next best thing would be to make my living as a news reporter. The problem I ran into there was that I wasn't good at economics; you needed to pass economics to enter "J" School. When I failed economics, I transferred to English and came out with a B.A. in English. I really wasn't suited for any kind of work when I landed in New York City. All my roommates were getting jobs in publishing houses and on newspapers and in advertising agencies. I was doing very badly because I had no skill, nothing to prepare me as they had from journalism school; and, worse, I was a girl who didn't know how to take shorthand. I can remember my father always warning me to learn shorthand if I wanted to be a success. In those days, a female who couldn't take shorthand and had no experience working at anything else was a poor thing; and that was me. I was a poor thing. I got the kind of job where my boss would say, "Now, when the phone rings, tell them your name, Mary Jane Meeker," as though I wouldn't remember my own name. By the way, Mary Jane Meeker is my own name. M.E. Kerr is the pseudonym I use for writing young adult novels. It's a play on my last name, Meeker—M. E. Kerr. I wandered from job to job; I had nine in my first year. I was always being fired. I wrote stories on my employer's time, because the jobs were so boring. Try being the assistant to the file clerk for a week sometime. I was often late because I stayed up late to write stories and slept through my alarm the next day. I began to feel pretty down as my roommates began advancing and I was off to the employment agency to look for still another job. I think now that not knowing shorthand was one of the best things that ever happened to me.

Because I couldn't get a good job, I was never interested in what I did for my paycheck; therefore, my interest in writing was never derailed; I kept right on—like a train.

My first break came when I sold a story to *Ladies Home Journal*. I took a look at the check, and I couldn't believe that anything I had written would be worth $75. I was right, too. It wasn't $75; it was $750! When my roommates came home from work, they saw the check and made me see the real figure, which I hadn't noticed because I was so excited. In those days, $750 was more than I made in two months, and it was more than my roommates made, too. From that moment on, I launched a campaign as a writer and sent out stories and also worked on an idea for an adult novel. A year after I got out of school, a publisher gave me a contract for my first novel, with a small advance. I sent him an outline, a chapter-by-chapter description of what I wanted my book to be about, and he called me and took me to lunch. He said he'd give me a thousand dollars while I worked on the novel and two more when it was finished. I was on my way. I wrote a lot of books under various pseudonyms, and I also used my own name occasionally. I admit I have sort of a soft spot for pseudonyms. I guess I like the romanticism of it. I remember when I was a kid posing as Eric Ranthram McKay, and maybe I just like the mystery of several names. I did write many mysteries under the name of Vin Packer.

After many years of writing for adults, I happened to read a book called *The Pigman*; Paul Zindel was the author. That was the first young adult book I had ever read when I felt afterwards that I'd like to try one of those. It's strange, too, in a way, because one of my dearest friends was Louise Fitzhugh, who wrote *Harriet, The Spy*. We talked a lot about writing together and she would always say, "Why don't you write a book for kids?" and I'd say, "I can't; I don't want to tiptoe around. I don't want to be careful of what I have to say because it's not an adult audience." Louise would get furious with me, and she'd say, "I never tiptoe around; I write everything I feel." And she did, too. She was one of the writers who made it possible for me to come along and tell a story straight and uncensored and true, the way she did, and was one of the first to do this in the field of young adult writing. Louise, by the way, had a crazy aunt who used to say to her, "Honey, always thank God you've got a talent, because you'll never have to work for a living." Her aunt, obviously, didn't think writing was work.

Writing is one of the most exciting and stimulating professions there is: it's spooky, too. There are times you think you are writing absolute rubbish and you might be writing something good. That's the rub.

There's some inner enemy at times who is out to tell you you are trash. You have to deal with that. I guess not just writers have to deal with that. We all have these inside characters putting us down; but because a writer is all by herself when she is writing, it's hard to stay convinced of her own worth while she forges ahead with a novel, for example. I know when I was writing my first book for young adults, *Dinky Hocker Shoots Smack*, I thought of throwing it away about a dozen times. The idea for *Dinky* came as a result of being a volunteer teacher in a New York City high school. The group of us, all of us writers, would go into the high schools one day a week and take over the English classes. These schools were mostly filled with ghetto kids who didn't read much at all and didn't write very well. We were supposed to get them interested in writing, so they would take an interest in reading. Mainly, we were supposed to tickle their imagination, get them to come out of themselves and express themselves. One of my brightest students was a fat girl named Tiny. She was so fat she needed two seats to sit on, and she was always talking through a mouth filled with Twinkies or M&Ms, and she was always giving me a rough time. But Tiny told the best stories of all, real horror stories about things like a woman swimming who swallowed a water snake and gave birth to a whole den of snakes. They were crazy, scary, impossible stories; always gory and bitter and brilliant. I began to print her stories in this little mimeographed publication with stories by the other students in the class, but Tiny was the star pupil in the class. Everyone loved her bizarre stories. We would all chorus after one of them, "Bizarre, Tiny," and she'd beam and write us another. I wasn't getting paid for these classes. I'm not, and never have been, a teacher. I had no real authority with the kids, so one day I got quite a jolt when this large, formidable, stern black woman confronted me as I was leaving the class. She was very angry looking. Her name was Mrs. Towers. "Who?" I said. "Mrs. Towers," she said, "Tiny's mother." Then she said, "I do not send my daughter to school so she can learn to write sick stories." I said, "They are very imaginative." She said, "They may be, but they are not what I want any daughter of mine to put down on paper." We started talking and she told me she worked very hard with a church group. She was a God-fearing, devout woman, and this was another reason she was so concerned. Tiny seemed so far from what she had been brought up to be. The more we talked, the more I realized Mrs. Towers spent most of her free time at the church helping other people's children, helping addicts, helping thieves, helping muggers. Helping, helping, helping, while home alone, eating herself into a whale out of loneliness and a feeling of rejection, was her

M.E. Kerr

daughter. Mrs. Towers didn't even perceive the name Tiny wasn't the greatest name for a girl who looked like an elephant, however affectionately she intended it. Mrs. Towers was like the woman who puts out a fire in the house across the street while her own house is smouldering. I never could forget Tiny, and gradually, she became an idea. I went over and over the idea trying to fix it for myself to write. I knew I couldn't write about Blacks. I am not a Black, and it's a special experience to grow up Black. I knew the story could come from "any people"—blue, green red, yellow, white; it was a very likely story.

I was living in Brooklyn Heights at the time and filled with learning about the Heights because I was new there. I decided to set the story there and have it happen in a middle-class white lawyer's family, have the mother be rehabilitating dope addicts in her spare time, and have the girl named Dinky. That was how it all started. It was the beginning of *Dinky Hocker Shoots Smack*. I thought about the book for about four months before I sat down and wrote it. It took three weeks to write. It has become one of my most successful books to date.

Sometimes, when I'm sitting out here in East Hampton, New York (I live not far from the ocean), when I'm staring out my study window wondering about things, in order to avoid writing, I think back and I wonder whatever would have happened if I had learned shorthand.

NORMA KLEIN

Interviewed by Paul Janeczko

BOOKS BY NORMA KLEIN

Blue Trees, Red Sky   Pantheon
Girls Can Be Anything   E. P. Dutton
Girls Turn Wives   Simon & Schuster (Ballantine)
Hiding   School Book Service (Pocket Books)
It's Not What You Expect   (Avon)
It's Okay If You Don't Love Me   (Dial)
Mom, the Wolf Man and Me   (Avon)
Sunshine   Harper and Row (Avon)
Taking Sides   (Avon)
What's It All About?   (Dial)

N.K. I have a very odd method of writing. I don't know whether I would recommend it or not; it just happens to work for me. I guess I was always scared of writing a novel. Maybe because I had studied Russian literature and all the novels run more than 2000 pages. So, for years I avoided it, and editors are never eager to publish short story collections; they are always asking you, "When are you going to write a novel?" One day I just decided—tomorrow you are starting a novel, and you must go in your study; and you must type ten pages a day, Monday through Friday, until you have reached page 300. And I did that. That, in a way, was the hardest one, because I just decided on a Monday, and Tuesday I began. Now, I would say when I write a book, I take notes sometimes a few months ahead of time—just little things in pencil about ideas for it. Somehow that seemed to work for me. I mean it overcame the self-doubt which I guess everyone feels. I'm very acutely aware of it. But even when you're on page one, all of a sudden you feel, "This is a terrible idea. Why am I writing it? I should give up." So this is a way of just forcing myself to get a finished manuscript produced, and it's varied. Sometimes the book has been printed more or less as it stood in that version. Sometimes the editor has suggested revisions; but I'm not as good as some writers are about revising my own work. That is, I type the ten pages in the morning and in the afternoon I will reread it and pencil in little notes in the margin. But it's hard for me to do a total revision without an editor saying, "There is a weakness here." or "Take this out." I'm always eager for an editor to give that kind of advice; it has been helpful.

P.J.   So you still write every day?

N.K,   I don't really write every day. No, because since, in a way, this is a rather rapid method, I would wind up writing too much, and I haven't found a solution to what to do in between writing, except go crazy. Maybe I should try to write something more slowly. I've also tried experimenting with different things; for instance, I once did a novelization called *Sunshine,* which was based on a television movie, and that was interesting to me because, here I was, giving someone else's story ideas and characters, but I had to flush it out and fill it in with my own feelings. I enjoyed that. I think I could do that kind of thing as well, if I had the chance.

P.J.   There was a sequel to that.

N.K.   I did the sequel. That was a little harder because the movie was based on a single screenplay by one woman (Carol Sobiewski). The sequel was not a movie; it was a TV series. Each script had been written by a different person and had very different tones and approaches. I found that was a little bit harder to unite into a coherent book than the earlier ones.

P.J.   Of the things that you have written, what is your favorite?

N.K.   I think it's always hard to say because you're influenced by the reception it's gotten; and I think probably my first book, *Mom, the Wolf Man and Me,* got the most enthusiastic response; so, in that way, I think maybe it's the best. At other times, I think I like the books that perhaps haven't done as well; they are just like the unfavored child to the outside world, whom you love the most. I enjoy writing humorous stories. Now, sometimes I think I have written a humorous book and no one else agrees. But my aim, I guess, if I could do anything, would be to be somewhat of a humorist, a realistic writer, but with humorous overtones. And I do like it when readers say, "You made me laugh out loud."

P.J. What is the essence of good writing?

N.K. I can only talk about the kinds of things I like in writing, because I think there isn't any single answer to that. I like the kind of writing that's very simple, where you don't stop and admire the sentence and say, "How beautifully written this is," but where you get involved with the characters. I happen not to care so much about plot myself. In fact, often I read the last chapter of a book first, so that I won't be in any suspense. I don't like being in suspense, and I always like reading a book for the second or third time more than the first time. Then I can go through it at a leisurely pace, and I find that's very enjoyable. And, as I say, I do like writers with a sense of humor; maybe not the kind that make you roll. I don't like heavies, that kind of southern Gothic type. I think I prefer a style like Hemingway or Chekhov, or someone who's just very simple, simple as can be.

P.J. Are there some humorists who have influenced you, or humorists whom you admire?

N.K. I always used to like Oscar Wilde as a teenager and George Bernard Shaw. They are both playwrights, but I feel that Wilde, particularly, had this thing of humor based on saying the opposite of what would usually be expected, and I found that appealing. I always liked Jane Austen very much. I don't know if she is still read as much today. Again, hers is a very subtle kind of humor but that's the kind I would be aiming for.

P.J. When you are writing a book, is theme a conscious effort on your part or do you just write a good story and then the theme comes from the plot?

N.K. I think I do have trouble with plot. I usually start with a situation let's say, in *Taking Sides*. In one of my books, I thought it would be an interesting idea to write about children who are living with their father rather than with their mother. The parents had been divorced, but rather than automatically living with the mother (in this case the father happened to be a writer who worked at home) it was easier for the children to live with the father. So I started with that; I really didn't know what was going to happen in terms of events in the course of the story. In another one, *It's Not What You Expect*, I had read in *The Times* about a group of teenagers who ran their own restaurant for one summer, and I just thought that was an interesting idea. I thought I would explore it, but it wasn't until I got into it that I filled in the relationship among the people.

P.J.   Can you think of specific people or specific writers who have influenced you?

N.K.   I do read all the time, and I think you can be influenced by a writer that you really admire tremendously. It happened when I was studying Russian literature. The writer I admired most was Chekhov, who had written a great many short stories and plays. But I think there's sort of a danger in trying to imitate a writer whom you admire, because, I think, one of the key things in writing is finding what your own style is going to be. It might be that you admire someone, but that's not your thing; and I felt that a little bit with Chekhov. After all, he is a nineteenth-century writer, and he writes in a way which just wouldn't be natural today. I think when people sometimes say, "If Tolstoy were writing today, would he write about sex as explicitly as people do today?" He probably would, because he couldn't be writing the same way he did then. I think one has to be, or just automatically is, in tune with one's particular era. For instance, I never thought of writing in the first person until I began writing for young people, and I realized that that came very naturally and had a kind of intimate quality which, I think, young people seem to enjoy. But if you had asked me earlier, I would have said, "Oh, the first person is not equal to the third person as a way of telling a story." You know, now I think any way is all right if it works; just be open to any method that exists.

P.J.   What advice would you give young people who want to become writers?

N.K.   I think some people have had interesting writing careers where they haven't started out writing, and I think one could do it either way. That is, there are people who have entered other professions and led interesting lives and then, in their forties, when they have had a good deal of experience in the outside world, they sit down to write. I think that's one way to do it. Or my way, which is that I haven't really ever done anything but writing, so I have a kind of wondering what the outside world is like. I guess whichever you pick, you probably think, "I would be so much better now if I had started earlier." But I think there is also something to be said about getting in touch with the outside world, learning about people in a broader sense than your own family. You can't say it as a rule, because there have been writers that have had jobs, and there have been writers that haven't. I don't think either way automatically produces better writing; but I also think it is important to somehow have some kind of self-confidence, which I instilled in myself just to do the ten-page-day thing. Just write it and try not to be self-critical. I think there are millions of people who could be writers in terms of the amount of talent they have, but they're so self-critical that either they never write the thing, or they will show it to one editor and, if it's turned down, they'll decide it's no good. When I was writing short stories, sometimes they would be taken the forty-fifth time I sent them out. The point is when they were published, no one knew, and then they might even be picked for an anthology for the best of the year. I think people just don't realize that rejection is something you face constantly. Just because you've been published once, twice, even ten times, doesn't mean that your book is going to be taken by the first person you show it to.

P.J. Do you have any advice in terms of the practical aspects of writing?

N.K. I happen to find it easier to write on a typewriter. Now, again, this is just a personal thing with me. I feel the advantage to that is when you come to rereading it the next day, it looks more objective somehow. You don't feel as caught up in your own self in a sense; and then you can always pencil in things in the margin. Plus, I think, one does think rather rapidly, and to me, the typewriter is a way of making it easier. I feel I can keep pace with my thoughts, whereas, when I'm writing, I feel that I have to slow down.

P.J. Is it necessary to write all the time? Write every day?

N.K. I don't think so. I don't. Probably there's a point in keeping at it in a general sense. I think everyone who writes would say, "Don't wait for inspiration; you have to go in there and just force yourself to do it." But I think that there are writers who might write just one book a year and work on it very intensively for a month or two; that would be their way. Then there might be others who would write one page a day; others who would say, "Take a certain number of hours and don't come out of your study until you've done that." I think the only danger in letting long gaps take place is that you start losing self-confidence. Maybe keeping at it, even if it's not working on one big thing, but alternating with stories or sketches or little things, is a good idea.

NORMA AND HARRY MAZER

Interviewed by Paul Janeczko

BOOKS BY NORMA FOX MAZER

A Figure of Speech   Delacorte (Dell)
I, Trissy   Delacorte (Dell)
Dear Bill, Remember Me? And Other Stories
    Delacorte (Dell)
Saturday, the Twelfth of October   Delacorte (Dell)

BOOKS BY HARRY MAZER

Dollar Man   Delacorte (Dell)
Guy Lenny   (Dell)
Snow Bound   Delacorte (Dell)

BOOKS BY NORMA FOX MAZER AND HARRY MAZER

The Solid Gold Kid   Delacorte (Dell)

P.J.   How does a husband and wife writing team operate?

H.M.   Probably by not considering themselves a writing team. I think that what we had to do very early was to separate ourselves.

N.M.   We really thought about this, whether we were going to be Norma and Harry Mazer or Harry and Norma Mazer, like Bill and Vera Cleaver, whom we consider practically as one person when we think of their books. I am not quite sure at the moment why we decided not to; maybe we were thinking of egos and perhaps Harry's ego more than mine, but at this moment, I would say that mine is very much involved. We are very glad we didn't decide to do that, because as it turned out, we both write with different styles, and what we bring to our books is very different. Actually, as a team, we just did our first book together, *The Solid Gold Kid.*

H.M. We've done seven books separately, and this is the first one together.

N.M. Yes. And that was a lot of fun, working together. There were no problems.

P.J. How do you go about writing a book with someone else?

N.M. We plan together—that's easy. We just talk, and you bat ideas back and forth. You have to be careful there. I have to remind myself every once in a while when I don't like an idea of Harry's not to say, "No, that's terrible." You have to be tactful at times and let an idea sit. You have to agree on everything. We did alternate chapters by drafting, so we had a well-planned book before we even began writing, which isn't always the case when you are working alone.

H.M. When you do a book together, it limits the type of book you can do. It tends to be more of a genre type of story, and that's the type of story we have done. The story line is very strong. It's a kidnap story. Actually, I have wanted to do a kidnap story for a number of years, and I had, more or less, worked out the plot and the plot persisted. Together, we developed the characters and a lot of the details of the story. We then took alternate chapters.

N.M. We worked over each other's draft material. Eventually, we arrived at one of the revisions. Then we would come to a place and feel, "This just isn't developed right," and one of us would take it off and write, and the other person would work it over. Then we would sit down together and that's pretty much the way we'd go about it.

H.M. In this kind of writing, it doesn't make too much difference who does the drafting; the revision changes it drastically. There is very little of the original material left, and we do it over as many times as is necessary.

P.J. Do you plan to do other books together?

N.M. Yes. After we do a book on our own, then we would like to do a book together. It's a relief; you don't get as involved; it doesn't come as much from your guts.

P.M.   When you're working on a book, Norma, do you bounce ideas off him, or do you just work by yourself?

N.M.   Both things go on. There's a period when we are talking about ideas. Yes, I would say, in a broad sense, we talk about ideas; it's very useful; it saves time, really, though we are so slow, I don't know what would happen if we didn't have each other to bounce ideas against.

H.M.   She's my editor when I am doing my own book; the first editor, before the publisher's editor gets to it. If she sees things that are wrong, she will read a draft; I'll write a draft and hand the draft to her. Many writers, from what I have read, will have to take a piece of writing and put it away when they work alone. Sometimes they have a relationship with editors or agents where they are able to hand this unformed material in and get some good editorial advice. But in our case, I think it is really a time-saver and it is wonderful. I know it's wonderful for me. I write a draft; I can give it to Norma and, in a week or so, I know what I have to do next.

P.J.   What is your writing routine like, Harry, in terms of the day-to-day business of writing?

H.M.   I am at my desk every day. At one time, I thought I could write all day long; I could write eight hours or ten hours, but what it's become and what is real is about three hours of creative work. Editorial work I can do over a longer period, and rewriting I can do over a longer period. It usually is from nine to twelve in the morning for the creative writing, but I will stay at my desk at least another two hours.

N.M.   He works with a constantly operating guilty conscience. He really stays at the desk longer than he should.

P.J.   What about your routine?

N.M.   Fortunately, we are both morning people, so our routines mesh, and for many years, they were dictated by the children, of course. We only have one left at home now, and she is very independent, which is nice, so we get to sleep late. There was a time when we actually got up at 3:30 in the morning for about a year. That was when we became very, very serious and started doing part-time writing, and we had four children. Harry was working in a factory, and I was working at home with the children. We were both trying desperately to write, and we finally realized one day that we were trying to write at the end of the day when we were both flat out physically. The kids were still going to bed fairly early, so we just started tucking in with them about 8:30 at night, and getting up at 3:30 in the morning. I think we did three hours before he went to work and the kids were up.

H.M.　I didn't want to give my best hours to that factory. I went in half asleep.

P.J.　How did you get started writing, Norma?

N.M.　I've always written, ever since I was a kid; not well, and I didn't have any guidance, but this is the only thing I could ever do. I couldn't play an instrument and I couldn't dance, and I am not an athlete, and all I could ever do was get a pat on the back from my English teachers, so I always wanted to write.

P.J.　Harry, what about you? How did you get started?

H.M.　I would say that I always wanted to write, but the burden that I suffered under was that I never thought that I could write, that I was not the equal of the models I had for myself. That, I think, gave me a writer's block before I was a writer. It was just difficult for me to put down one word after another, and I couldn't imagine I could write. But when I wrote something, it was credible; it was well-received in school, but I just couldn't get past the burden I put on myself. What finally liberated me was that time when I finally left factory work and said, "This is what I am going to do." I was forced to write to live, and was forced to write many, many words. I could no longer worry about building walls. I had to do the scenes; I had to do short stories; the developments were just too big to allow me to worry about each word.

P.J.　What is the essence of good writing? You mentioned models that you had.

H.M.　I would say simplicity is a big component. I would say that having a story and telling your story with clarity is very important. A writer should also avoid sham. I think this is one of the big dangers that writers often suffer from. For example, you may be showing off or putting on or worrying that you are not fancy enough in your presentation. I think you have to be honest; you believe in what you are writing. In other words, you have something that you want to say. You tell your story and you are not above your writing; you are not above your audience. I think in the juvenile field, generally, this is one of the dangers; the danger of patronizing, the danger of writing down. You see less and less of this in the writing of recent years, but you do still come across it. I would say that is the big thing that you have to avoid because it is always detected, and you don't get away with it. You suffer from it, and the writing suffers from it.

P.J. Where do you get the ideas for your books?

N.M. The book, *Dear Bill, Remember Me?* is eight short stories and I would say a number of the ideas came out of things that happened to me or to people I knew. I have a story in there about a girl who is dying of cancer, and I had a friend who died of cancer many years ago. But I would say that, basically, that's where the resemblance of the story ends. But that's about all you need. I need something real, some core. I'm never quite sure what it's going to be; it could be something as momentous as this—having a friend die—but it could also be just a phrase that I've heard that sticks in my mind, and I start spinning from there. I don't analyze why something stays with me and something else doesn't.

H.M. The idea for a story or book is only the opening; I once compared it to a string or rope that is coming out of the ground: you get hold of the end of it and that's the idea. What you get at the beginning is not necessarily what you are going to have at the end, but it's enough to get you going. This, of course, is individual, when we are writing our own books. When we are working together, we don't operate in that way. The idea is much more developed; there aren't as many surprises.

P.J. What about *Dollar Man*? How did that come about?

H.M. There is a lot of the autobiographical element in *Dollar Man*. I was a bad boy and I lived a lot of fantasy. Fantasy, of course, all had to do with somehow miraculously shedding all this bad and emerging as a beautiful person. I remember sitting in an auditorium when I was in high school and having this fantasy, dreaming about myself as a man in armor; that's too glamorous an image, but that's the idea. Some of the elements that appear have to appear in order for the book to take form; the element of having a single parent, the father being missing, having to search for the father.

N.M. That's what started it; the idea actually had to do with the boy and his father at the very beginning, before Mark emerged as a character.

H.M. Right. And the boy and his father seem to be something that I am very much interested in. I deal with it in my first book, *Guy Lenny*. It is about a boy living with his father and his mother comes home. In *Snow Bound*, I didn't deal with it at all; I did a straight adventure story; in *Dollar Man*, it was the boy living with his mother who becomes enormously interested in discovering things about his father. In the book that I am contracted to write, I again deal with father and son. It is another relationship between father and son. That, of course, is what I have to write out of myself.

P.J.   Is theme a conscious effort on your part, or do you begin with the story and theme becomes a part of that story?

H.M.   Well, you take *Snow Bound*, it didn't start with theme. There, I know very clearly how the book began. First of all, I was always interested in looking for some aspect of a *Robinson Crusoe* story, a survival story. There was an article in *Life Magazine* some years ago, and it was about a couple of hunters in Idaho who went out one fall and got caught in a snowstorm; they were stranded for almost two months; one died and one survived. That started me going with that story. You just can't tell the story—there has to be some meaning. What is the story all about? This is where you get the theme, and I had to get the theme in *Snow Bound*, as I've had to get the theme in every book I have written.

N.M.   I think a lot of times it's implicit and you actually don't recognize it, but I find it's impossible to write without knowing what I am writing about means. You have to know what your writing means, and it directs everything that happens. You can have a story, but without meaning to it, it's an anecdote. To tell a story without meaning leaves the reader completely unsatisfied.

P.J.   What do you owe your readers?

N.M.   I think I owe them a good story, and I always hope for that. I'd love it if people would tell me. For instance, I had a letter from a young girl about *Saturday, the Twelfth of October*. She said her teacher gave it to her and she picked it up and started reading it; and she kept reading it through study hall and took it home and stayed up late to finish it. She said she couldn't put it down and, of course, that, to me, is the greatest compliment going. I love it. I think the element of honesty, which is just so subjective, has to do with one's own feeling. You know when you are being dishonest in the writing. For myself, I always want to write the best book I can; I am never satisfied. It is very difficult for me, once a book is published, even to look at it. It takes me several years to look at it without cringing. And I go through these awful periods where I just wonder why I wrote this, and why I brought this out so that everyone can see how terrible it is. I think we all go through that. There is a certain point at which I just feel marvelous when the ideas start coming, and I have these fantastic egomaniacal feelings that this masterpiece is coming out. However, that doesn't last too long, and the other feelings start coming—that I am caught up in this terrible thing I am writing and

I don't know why I am doing it, and all that sort of thing. But, underneath that, I want to do the very best I can. I do owe it to my readers, but I owe it to myself as much as anything. What impels me as much as anything is my own sense of pride, self-desire to be a decent writer.

P.J. Can you think of specific people or writers who have influenced you?

N.M. No. I read everything, including *Nancy Nurse*, from one through twenty-nine, when I was a kid; and *Robinson Crusoe*; and just anything that was in the house, I read my parents' books, our books, anything in the library. Of course, there are certain writers I love, and when I come across a writer that I particularly like, I feel that's what I would like to do. I like some of Jessamyn West's books, for instance, and what I love is the combination of literacy and popularity she has; the stories she tells, and yet the high degree of intelligence I feel she brings to the work. I think that's great.

P.J. Harry? Anyone who has influenced you?

H.M. I would give practically the same answer that Norma gave. I do feel, though, that everything I read, good or bad, whether I like it or not, helps me, influences me, and in that sense, everything I read I find influences me. Now, the book that we just did, *The Solid Gold Kid*, the kidnap story influenced me in this way: I read a kidnap story—I won't mention the author—in the field; not *the* kidnap story, but one that was done within the past twenty years, and I disliked it. I didn't like anything about it. Then I said, "I can do a better book than that." In that sense, that's my influence.

N.M. It's negative/positive.

H.M. Right.

P.J. Would either of you have any advice for young people who are interested in becoming writers?

N.J. Yes. Write! Somebody should have taken me by the hand when I was young and told me to just keep writing a journal, if nothing else. Our youngest daughter does that and, if nothing else, it's a marvelous satisfaction to go back to it and read it. She sits down and reads her journal from a couple of years ago and just thinks it's great. She's in love with her own writing. But if you want to write, you must write, because that is what we had to learn. When we finally got around to it, we were adults; we had children; we just did it in the hardest possible way. As

Harry was saying before, we wrote pulp for a living for many years because we wanted to write, and it was a great thing to do. It was training, and we wrote millions of words a year, and those millions of words taught us an awful lot. So write whatever you feel is useful; write letters, write in your journal. A lot of kids like to write poetry. They should write poetry. A lot of things I noticed with our own children is that they suffer from the same thing Harry was talking about. They are intensely critical of themselves as they write, and they feel that each word they put down has to be right. Of course, we constantly say, "Just write it down and then go back, and the next time you do it, it's going to be so much better. Don't worry about the first time. Just get it out. Don't worry about your English; don't worry about your grammar; don't worry about your spelling; don't worry about anything. Just try and write down what it is you want to say." That's what is important.

H.M.   I think that becoming a writer is so extremely difficult. Desire is not enough, but desire, of course, is basic.

N.M.   Half the world has the desire.

H.M.   Right. Everybody you meet says, "Oh, if I only had the time and your discipline, I'd write." Even as they say it, they hardly know what they are saying. I think that in order to really persist, the person has to have a need to write or find pleasure in writing. It isn't always a pleasure. You often wonder why you ever persist; but there is something that is compelling in the writing. Then I would emphasize what Norma just said—if you are writing, continue to write, and try to write without being critical. Get it down on paper and then put it away; take it out, look at it, and change it. Or you can throw it away and write something else.

MILTON MELTZER

Interviewed by Paul Janeczko

BOOKS BY MILTON MELTZER

A Light in the Dark: The Life of Samuel Gridley Howe
Harper and Row
*In Their Own Words: A History of the American Negro
1619-1965* (Three Volumes)   T.Y. Crowell (Apollo)
Langston Hughes: A Biography   Crowell (Apollo)
Margaret Sanger: Pioneer of Birth Control   Harper
and Row
Never to Forget: The Jews of the Holocaust   Harper
and Row (Dell)
Thaddeus Stevens and the Fight for Negro Rights
Harper and Row
Underground Man   (Dell)
World of Our Fathers   (Dell)

P.J.   Where do you get the ideas for your books? How do you decide
what to write about?

M.M.   That varies considerably. Some of the ideas come out of the
reading I've done; some come from the books I have already worked on
where I may run across an interesting event, or incident, or character
that stimulates me to write something in greater detail about that
person. Some ideas come out of your own life experiences. For instance,
I recently did a book on the WPA Arts Projects of the 1930s that's partly
autobiographical because I worked on the Federal Theatre Project in
those years—my first job after college—and long after decided to do a
book about it.

P.J. Your latest book on the Jewish experience and what the Jewish people went through, how long did it take you to write that book?

M.M. It took about a year, I think.

P.J. Now, does this include research? And how exactly do you go about writing a nonfiction book, this book in particular?

M.M. It requires a tremendous amount of reading. To begin with, I built myself a master bibliography of a good many of the books that have been written about the holocaust, by no means definitive, since the literature is enormous; but I got together what seemed to be the basic titles, and especially those that contained first person experiences: the memoirs, the journals, the diaries, and letters from people who survived the holocaust. I read them and gradually from that began to build an outline for my book that took shape in my head as the experiences moved me.

P.J. What gave you the idea to write that book?

M.M. That book came out of a very specific experience; it's not always easy to pinpoint it that way. My wife had brought home from the university, where she works, a pamphlet commenting on books about the holocaust for people from junior high school level all the way up to graduate school, or adult level, and the key point it made was that the holocaust was terribly scant or ignored, which astonished me; and I decided I'd like to do something in my own way and try to rectify that.

P.J. Once you have your research, you've done your reading, you have your outline, where do you go from there? What is your writing routine?

M.M. I find morning hours are most productive for me; I think they afford the greatest amount of energy, though other writers are just the reverse and write at night. I rise early and get to the desk. I write in longhand and, usually, if I'm at the state of writing as distinct from the research, I can write four or five hours straight. By the end of that time you are worn out. It's a physically and emotionally wearing experience whether you are writing fiction or nonfiction. The afternoons I usually give to reading rather than writing.

P.J. Are you working on more than one project at a specific time?

M.M. I often am. Since I write chiefly nonfiction, once I've reached the stage of writing the book and have finished the research, I may spend those afternoons I have just spoken of beginning the research for the book that's coming up next.

P.J. Do you do a lot of rewriting?

M.M. Yes, I do. I write in longhand first, and do a tremendous amount of hacking and rehacking and reworking and throwing sheets away, and at the end of each day, or at the beginning of the next day, I type up what I have written in longhand the day before, or the hours before, and then I rework that. Usually, most things go through, I'd say, two or three drafts at least.

P.J. In your opinion, what is the essence of good writing?

M.M. I think, to speak in your own true voice, and that's the hardest thing to find. I never think mechanically of something that people label "style." Whatever that may be comes out of your own experience, and the influences you have been subject to, as a reader first of all, from your early years on. On paper you really find out what you think and what you feel; you often don't know that until you try to put it down on paper. Sometimes you are very much surprised about what emerges.

P.J. Can you think of specific people in your past, or perhaps writers, who have influenced you?

M.M. Well, I can think of a teacher I had to whom I am tremendously grateful. When I was a high school student in Worcester, Massachusetts, I had a marvelous English teacher named Anna C. Shaughnessy, who was a tremendously stimulating woman, very demanding on what we read, and a great critic of what we wrote as students, too. She opened up my eyes to the breadth and depth of literature as a marvelous experience. Many years later, I dedicated one of the books I wrote to her; I was so grateful.

P.J. What about writers? Are there writers who influenced you?

M.M. I suppose there are. You are inevitably influenced by the people you read, and the younger you are, the more influenced you are, I think. It takes time to break away from that, as I suggested before, to find your own voice. I don't think I could put my finger on any one writer.

P.J. Were you interested in reading and writing when you were in school?

M.M. Yes. I was what people call "a good student," I guess, and enjoyed school. In fact, at first I wanted to be a teacher; I didn't think of being a writer. But, by the time I was in college, I began to sell articles and stories to newspapers and magazines, and seeing my name in print made me decide: I like that. And I have continued writing ever since.

P.J. What got you started writing in the first place?

Interviewed by Paul Janeczko   69

M.M. I guess part of it was dictated; you had to write in school. You were always asked to do themes and papers and articles, and I found I enjoyed it. I worked for my school paper in junior and senior high school, and again I did it in college. Although I didn't make my living full-time as a writer at first—I had a variety of other jobs—writing was always involved as a tool for making a living, and a good many years later I was able to write books exclusively and not have to hold another job to make a living.

P.J. What do you feel you owe your readers?

M.M. Honesty, first of all, I think, to try to tell the truth about life and the world as you see it, and as honestly as you can. That isn't always easy to do, because you're not always sure of your own feelings and, of course, your understanding of the world you live in changes as you change, as you grow older, or as your experiences vary. I know I've changed my mind about a number of things. At one time, I used to feel a little guilty about it, if the idea was good then, it should be stuck to forever; but I realize that was a terrible mistake.

P.J. How about the writing itself? You owe readers the truth first of all, but what else do you owe them as a writer?

M.M. I think you have the obligation of conveying what you think you have to say, as clearly and as effectively as possible and that, of course, involves the craft of writing itself.

P.J. How do you go about doing it? Can that craft be learned?

M.M. I think so. I don't think you can learn talent; I think you have to have some knack, some flair, some quality, perhaps, that you are born with. But I think a tremendous amount can be done on that substratum to build a craft and to build a skill, and you can learn that mostly by just hard work, sitting down and writing all the time. I think that it's just nonsense that you wait for inspiration. It takes a lot of sweat, and I found early when I began writing full-time that I had to go to my desk every day and write, whether I felt like it or not. You find that once you start, it begins to flow after awhile; something gets going, and you learn, of course, the more you do. Presumably, you keep learning from your own mistakes and from reactions to your work, and hopefully, you do better the next time.

P.J. Is there any reason why you work with nonfiction primarily?

M.M. I don't know what accounts for that, except that I very rarely wrote poetry, or attempted to write poetry or fiction, even as a student in grade school or high school or college; it seemed always to be

Milton Meltzer

nonfiction. The one exception is a novel I did a few years ago which is a historical novel, *Underground Man*, and that really started as nonfiction and was then converted to fiction.

P.J.   What advice would you give young people who want to become writers?

M.M.   First, do a good deal of reading, read a great variety of writers, not with the notion of trying to imitate them—but they do convey something of their own sense of life, their own sense of values—and then to write and write and write.

P.J.   You find it essential that you have a routine, that you write every day?

M.M.   Yes, I think that's vital; and it's got to the point now where I even feel uneasy on weekends or if I go away on a vacation and I am remote from a place where I can write. I miss it very much.

P.J.   Can you give a case history of your book *Never to Forget?*

M.M.   If you mean from the point of view on how it was written, I think I could. When I went to work on *Never to Forget*, it was with the idea of trying to provide young people, particularly of junior and senior high school age, with a deeper understanding of the origins of the holocaust. There have been a number of very good novels about the experience of the holocaust written for young people, some based on personal experience and others purely imagined experience. But there has been almost nothing trying to deal with the holocaust. Some writers have tried to explain it historically. What were the roots of the holocaust? How did such a dreadful thing on so enormous and unbelievable scale come to pass? In the book, for that reason, I decided very early on it could be divided into three basic parts: one dealing with the deeper roots of anti-Semitism way back to the early Christian fathers two thousand years ago; then the modern part dealing with the rise of anti-Semitism in Germany in the nineteenth century; the second part of the book dealing with the holocaust experience itself and, there, as well as throughout the book, I chose to use the technique that combines narrative history, a chronological account of what happened, and an explanation of why it happened, intermixed with the experiences of the people who make that history, who lived that history. And from both sides—the victims and the people who do the victimizing. Wherever I could, I sought for letters, journals, diaries, notebooks, eyewitness accounts, testimony before such commissions as the Nuremberg Trial, or the trial of Eichmann which took place later, so that the young reader, particularly, would get some notion of how it felt to be alive at that time, and to be a part of this thing. Of course, it's authentic; nothing could be more authentic, so that the reader is moved in and out of the personal and from the personal on to the broader canvas, so that the personal gets a decent setting for it. The third part of the book deals entirely with the resistance of the Jews to what Hitler attempted to do to them and, unfortunately, succeeded, for the most part. My own historical research led me to the conviction that it's very much a myth that the Jews did not resist what was done to them; that they were led like sheep to the slaughter. I discovered from my reading that there was resistance of a great many kinds all the way from passive and spiritual resistance to taking up of arms, and to illegal methods of resistance, which I think are justified in that context. That's the last part of the book. To do a book like that, which involves a tremendous amount of reading, there's a very big bibliography at the back, which doesn't even include everything I read, that proved impossible to include in the book, but the major things, the things that were most influential in shaping my own thinking. My method of working is to take notes as I go along on those 3x5 little pads you get in the five and ten, and at first, I just pile them up. They usually contain only an idea I got from my reading or a reference if I think I may want to quote a passage, or go back to get more details later. After I have done a certain amount of reading, the book begins to take shape in my mind, and I start to sort those slips out on my desk, either by idea or varying theme; or sometimes if it moves that fast, by chapter, what seems a likely chapter structure. When I finish the research and have come to the actual stage of writing, the slips have all been filed in my desk according to chapter, and I'll pull those out and rearrange them on my desk to fulfill what I think is a valid way of treating the material of that one chapter. There I have very much in mind the shape, the structure, and form for the chapter. I want to get some means of catching the reader's attention very early on. Once you pass the first chapter, there has to be a beginning that links it with what went before, so there is a lot of weighing and balancing and judging, and it is as artistic, I think, as one would do if one were writing this as fiction. When the slips are arranged, I simply start writing in longhand, painfully, and then make these innumerable decisions any writer must make, if he takes his work seriously—if they are to use fact "a" against the facts "b," "c," or "d." You know your book is going to be of a certain length; you can't go on writing forever, and you can't bore readers by overdoing it. So you are faced with decision-making, which really is, I

Milton Meltzer

think, the essence of artistic judgment, and many times it's unconscious; you don't stop to think this weighs so much in the balance as against that. But you instinctively sense that this slip has something more important in it for your reader at this point than ten other slips that are on your desk and you put the others aside. My own technique of doing this is that once I have used the slip, I just strike a slash pencil mark through it, and put it in the file, together with the other slips that I didn't use, so that when and if I come back to rewrite, I may decide I made a mistake the first time; it doesn't read as well as I thought it should, or as effectively. I then have the option of looking at what I rejected, and that may come back into the book.

P.J. You made a comparison between the actual writing of a non-fiction book and the writing of a novel. Can nonfiction be considered a legitimate art form?

M.M. Well, I certainly think it can. It is hard for someone like myself who is writing nonfiction now to make any claims to art for myself, but I know there are other people writing whose work I value enormously for young people and I think it's as artistic as the best prize-winning novels. If one went back historically one could give unassailable examples of that: Boswell's *Life of Johnson* is a massive biography, and it is considered one of the world's literary masterpieces; or Henry Davis, or Rose Walden, which you can call either philosophical writing or nature writing; nonfiction fits into a number of genres and it's considered one of the greatest achievements in the English language. Or *The Decline and Fall of the Roman Empire*, to take an example in the field of history which, from the moment it appeared, has been acknowledged to be a masterpiece. I think it is proper to consider imagination as an aspect of creativity, but to think it can have sway or play only in fiction is a mistake. Your imagination is involved in every aspect of writing nonfiction, if you take your work seriously and are not doing hack work.

P.J. Why is nonfiction not given the exposure then that fiction receives?

M.M. I think possibly because of the nature of our education from early school on. I think most teachers and librarians, too, I am afraid to say, tend to think too narrowly that only fiction or poetry can be considered an artful form of writing. I think if they open their eyes a little wider and stretch their horizons and look at the kinds of examples I've given (and there are thousands of them—I gave only two or three), they would realize that they are doing an injustice to this form of writing. And I think it would upgrade the level of nonfiction writing for young people, too, if they were given that encouragement—if teachers, librarians, and judges of literary contests and so on, acknowledge that it's just as much in the running as fiction.

P.J.   Do you see a change in that attitude?

M.M.   In one or two cases, prizes that were given just for the best writing for young people and which were almost invariably given to fiction, that's begun to shift. In the case of the Boston Globe Horn Book Annual Award, they created a second category for nonfiction; they now give a prize for nonfiction and a prize for the best fiction.

P.J.   You would like to see other organizations do the same thing?

M.M.   Yes. The prizes are just a symbol of what I am getting at. I would really like to see teachers and librarians pay far more attention to this as a worthy form of writing.

Milton Meltzer

NICHOLASA MOHR

Interviewed by Paul Janeczko

BOOKS BY NICHOLASA MOHR

El Bronx Remembered   Harper and Row (Bantam)
In Nueva York   Dial
Nilda   Harper and Row (Bantam)

P.J. How did you get started writing?

N.M. I got started writing four years ago, and it was something that happened quite unexpectedly. All my life, I had made communication through visual vocabularies as I was a painter and a graphic artist for eighteen years. I studied very hard; first I did oil paintings, drawings, acrylics, and I used tempera; and then I was fascinated with print-making. As a fine artist, I never did commercial art. I managed to learn the art of printmaking, which is very specific; and you need to know a lot of technical steps to do an etching, because you work on metal, you work on stone. I did etching, embossing, lithography; and I did silk screening. I got very involved in that kind of work and I was not doing badly, because it takes a lot to be a starving artist, simply because you have to buy materials. You say, "Should I get a loaf of bread or a tube of paint or something for my work?" I had gotten a grant and, at this point in my life, I bought a big press, a big, beautiful electric press, which is what every print-maker's dream is—to have his own press. I put it up in my attic, and set up my studio, and I had an art agent, because fine artists depend on collectors. Having a gallery is no big deal; they can give you a showing, and you can come out selling absolutely no drawing. Unless it's a gallery that buys your stuff and gives you a salary, which is something only a few do (maybe a dozen or two fine artists have this privilege), you have to depend on collectors, that is, people who buy your work as you create it and finish it. I was with an art agent who discovered that one of my collectors was a publisher—not Harper and Row, another publisher. They said they had heard me speak and I had a lot of graffiti—long before graffiti became so popular in certain areas, expecially New York. They said, "Nicholasa, why don't you write about your experiences because you are from a particular group of Americans—Puerto Ricans—and there is so little written about them." My experiences were developed in my work. You could see them in my figurative work and the way I use colors. Sometimes I told a story through the visual interpretation and, hopefully, evoked feelings from the viewer. So this particular publisher who had collected my work said, "Have Nicholasa write fifty pages." I really wasn't interested; I was not a writer. I always liked to write; I had never had any difficulty writing. Some people play the piano. I can't, but I can write. So they continued bringing the subject up. Once I had a little bit of time, and I decided, well, why not? I'll sit down and write fifty pages. So, in the first person, I wrote about fifty pages, or a little less, in vignette form: what it was like to grow up as a young American Puerto Rican in the United States, in relationship to other Americans around you, and to be so economically deprived as I was as a youngster, and yet to have such a strong culture. My publisher liked it very much, but she didn't feel that it was quite what she wanted. I think what she expected was something much more sensational, the sort of stereotypical ghetto person. So I told her that much to my embarrassment I had never stolen anything, taken hard drugs, been raped or mugged. So I guess she thought my life was uneventful. I took back my vignettes and said, "Later." I went back to my art. Then I got a call from Harper and Row asking if I were interested in doing a cover for one of their books. While I was really not interested in commercial art, I came with my vignettes, and Ellen Rudin, who was my editor then, encouraged me to write and make these vignettes into a novel. I took out the first person form because it was too much of a confessional when you write I, I, I, and decided if I took it into the third person, I could take my experiences and base my plot and feeling on that. Then I could go further because I could narrate, I could step outside for character. Then I got a contract, and I wrote the first book, *Nilda*, which was put out by Harper. So that is how it happened. Then I fell very much in love with writing. At first, I was a little bit nervous; it was like getting a divorce. I did the cover jacket for the hard-back and I did eight illustrations, because I just couldn't accept the transition that I could write so easily after all those years. I found that I

Nicholas Mohr

could do certain things in writing and there was a crying need for what I had to say as a Puerto Rican, as someone living here, and as a woman.

P.J. For instance?

N.M. For instance, visual art is very much like music; it is very immediate. You sort of recognize. It's like when you hear a piece coming through, you immediately relate to that; unless it's an opera, which has words. You can hear that music coming through you, and many times, with art, it has to be an immediate sort of response to color, to space, to linear forms. What I could do with writing is be very specific; I could tell a story, really tell a story, and I could make people laugh. I could make people aware of what it was like for myself at the time. It was almost like a catharsis, the first book. I was even thinking of going into sculpture, but all of a sudden I found a medium where I was really comfortable. I could draw a picture with words, and it was extremely stimulating and eye-opening to realize what one could do with words. I see fiction as an art form which I don't see myself as leaving. Everything I have done as an artist is transferable to a new craft. I don't consider myself a novice, but I do consider myself someone who is learning a new craft.

P.J. What is the essence of good writing?

N.M. Well, for me, I don't write for young people, per se. I write for people. Some of them are young and some of them are old. I don't like this division that young people sort of have a place; they're people. There's a certain freshness when they see the world, so that a young person reading my work can identify, and an old person can go back into an odyssey of time. Good writing is when it affects everybody. I feel that my books can be read by everyone. They're not from nine to twelve, or eleven to whatever. I feel you have to learn to read and write. Once you learn to read, you can read my books; I write very, very simply, no matter how complex my message may be. I like a simple vocabulary that anyone can read, and I have had older people reading my work. I'm very excited that younger people read my work and like it, because I feel that's part of life, that's part of being alive. But good writing is writing that someone picks up and says, "Okay, I want to go on with this, not because it's for a teenager or adolescent, but because the writer is saying something that I want to get involved with."

P.J. What do you owe your readers?

N.M. I owe my readers the same thing I owed the people who looked at my graphics; that is, I owe them first, a certain amount of honesty towards the product that I am trying to finish. If I finish a product, it's got to be totally honest, devoid of banality, and it's got to be something that I can live with, and something that I feel they can get into. If they can't, they can't. Not everyone can love you. But it's as honest and straight as possible. If I say I'm starting a subject, no matter how difficult that subject might be, I have to see it through. I have to come to some sort of conclusion and commit myself. And it is a total commitment, whether it's a book or canvas or print; and the viewer can feel that. If the viewer wants to reject it, that's okay; but the commitment is there. That's what I feel, basically, I owe anyone who is looking at my work or reading my work.

P.J.   Is theme a conscious effort on your part, or do you start by telling a good story, and theme fits into that?

N.M.   I think they are related; you almost cannot separate them. There are times when the theme is important, and sometimes when it's unimportant; but I don't think it's terribly conscious with me. I feel that the story line or the theme is only an aspect of the writing. It's how the characters begin to breathe and how real they are. People are very important to me in my stories.

Nicholas Mohr

RICHARD PECK

Interviewed by Paul Janeczko

P.J.   How did you get started writing?

R.P.   I got started writing because I was a teacher in the seventh grade, and I couldn't find books about the experiences of kids that age to use in my classrooms and to recommend to my students for their independent reading.

P.J.   Where do you get the ideas for your books? How do you decide what to write about?

R.P.   That is an often-asked question. There is no one source for writing and for ideas; but, of course, my general source is what young people read. I stand behind them in paperback book stores and see what they take down off the shelves; I ask their librarians. Most of my novels are not from experience, but from observation. When I was teaching seventh graders, as I mentioned before, I was very curious about the friendships in seventh grade. They never seemed to last. So I wrote a book called *Dreamland Lake* about the friendship of two seventh grade boys and what kills that friendship at the end of that year.

P.J. So you do not write from your own experience?

R.P. I don't think I do; I think I write from my observation. I don't write my own youthful experiences, because they would be out of date, and I don't believe in self-expression. Nobody wants to read your diary except your mother.

P.J. What about your writing routine? What is that like?

R.P. It's pretty hectic. I travel about a quarter of the time, going around and talking to young people in libraries and schools, to teachers, and to librarians. When I come home, I am always confronted by a deadline. I write very slowly at the beginning; then, after I have written forty pages, I find that I am committed. I have put too much time into it not to finish it. Then I start working faster and faster, harder and harder, seven days a week. At the beginning, I will walk very carefully around a book idea and, frequently, I'll stop on page ten; but I never stop on page forty-one. Then I keep going.

P.J. Do you do a lot of rewriting?

R.P. Yes. I write every book about seven times. The saying that easy writing makes hard reading is true. I never can get it right the first six drafts. Then, I have to translate it from the speech of my age group to the speech of my readers.

P.J. What is the essence, in your opinion, of good writing?

R.P. The essence of good writing, it seems to me, is not so much what you say, but how you say it; how true do the speech patterns sound? How real is the situation? How entertaining is the story? Not all stories are laughs or comedies; but all stories must entertain somehow. Not all books do.

P.J. Is theme a conscious effort, or do you merely try to tell a good story and let the theme surface within the story?

R.P. Theme is a conscious effort. The theme is the reason you wrote the book. The plot never is. The characterization isn't, usually. But the theme, the underlying truth behind the story, is the most important aspect and that, for me, comes first. Now, other themes surface as you write; but the basic theme is there to begin with. For example, I wrote a book called *Representing Super Doll*, on the topic of glamour. Well, the theme of that book is the terrible tyranny of glamour, not only when you don't have it but when you do. And then the story evolves: a sort of funny, midwestern story about a girl who's won so many beauty contests she doesn't have a friend left. The theme is to make young people question their own standards of what is beautiful, what is socially acceptable.

P.J. What do you feel you owe your readers?

R.P. Entertainment and truth. Young people, in fact most people, won't read anything unless they are entertained on some level, and I can't write through a book without believing in its truth. This can be a very light truth or it can be a very heavy one. I have written a book called *Are You in the House Alone?* and I have written it because the typical victim of the crime of rape is a teenage girl in our country. That's a very hard truth. Yet, I wanted my readers to know some things about this crime, that our laws are stacked against the victim and in favor of the criminal. I wanted them to know some of the medical aspects of this problem, and I also wanted them to know what it's like to be a victim. I had to do a lot of research and interview a lot of people and go to a lot of places. I had to talk to doctors and lawyers and police personnel and victims. I had to deal only in the truth. I couldn't put a happy ending on this story because we don't have any happy endings to this problem in our society. Now where does entertainment come into all that? The tension, the characterization, the suspense in the story that lead you into it so that you can find out the truth.

P.J. Why did you choose to write that particular book?

R.P. Because I had read a number of nonfiction books on the subject of rape; they alerted me to the problem. They made me realize what fears women live with in our society, and how wrong our laws are, and how badly implemented they are. And then, when I read in every one of those adult books that the typical victim was a teenage girl, I realized that these future victims were my readers, and I had something to say to them. I wanted them to know. The theme of that book expanded at the end. It wasn't just a story about one kind of crime. It became a story of what it is like to be a former victim in our society. How do you go on living after you have been an entry on a police blotter? Who are your real friends? They show up afterwards. What are your real relationships with other people? Our society is filling up with victims of all kinds of crimes, and we don't seem to be very interested in them. I am.

P.J. Was there a specific person who influenced you or inspired you to become a writer?

R.P. Yes, I think so. It was the student body when I was a teacher. You can never think of being a writer until you know who your readers are, and your readers almost always are going to be strangers—people who are not like you. In my case, they were people who were not my age, who didn't have my interests, necessarily, but I was interested in them, and in communicating with them. A teacher has to communicate with people every day, or he isn't doing his job. That's the best background for writing I can imagine.

P.J.   What would you do if you were not a writer?

R.P.   I can't imagine. I've only been a writer for six years; before that, I was a teacher. I don't think I'd go back to teaching. Teaching isn't what I wish it were. If I had my life to live over, I would take a degree in journalism and approach writing through newspaper work. In our society, three fields have provided an incredible number of writers in this century: Teaching, newspaper work, and advertising. I guess the reason for that is that these three fields depend upon communicating with strangers; deadlines and meeting them; and using evocative, good, interesting language.

P.J.   Do you do other kinds of writing besides novels?

R.P.   Yes. I write for adults in the nonfiction area on architecture and I write a column in the *New York Times* on the architecture of New York City, its history, and its neighborhoods. One of the most difficult problems of communicating with young people is that they don't know enough history and geography, so it's very hard to know where to set your novel. When you're writing about local history and architecture to adults, you know that.

P.J.   What advice would you give young people who want to become writers?

R.P.   I would advise them to learn ten new words every day they live. To write without having an adequate vocabulary is hopeless. To write the way you really speak is hopeless because you have to speak in hundreds of voices when you are creating voices. It's very much like writing a play and then performing in it yourself. You have to take all the parts, so you have to know how all kinds of people talk—waitresses in restaurants, college professors, parents, small children, adolescents. You've got to handle slang and foreign languages and accents. Becoming more language-conscious is the most important thing to a writer because, until he has the vocabulary, he has nothing but frustration.

P.J.   What do you find young people want from their reading?

Richard Peck

R.P.   I find they want supernatural powers, escape, all kinds of strange romance, and what seventh graders call "gore." I thought at first, when I heard that, that I didn't have anything to offer. But if they want gore, I'll give it to them. I have written a novel called *The Ghost Belonged to Me* and a new one called *Ghosts I Have Been*, which deal, in part, with the supernatural. Now that doesn't relate to the theme. The theme is something else, but the surface, the story, the plot, deal in the supernatural. I wasn't interested in the supernatural until I found out how interesting it is in the eighth and ninth grades and how long a life Edgar Allan Poe had. I'd like to have a long life like that, too.

P.J.   Of the books you have written, which one is your favorite?

R.P.   That one I just mentioned, *The Ghost Belonged to Me. It's my* favorite because it has been very well received by readers, and because it deals with a theme I like—a young boy just entering the world and an old man just leaving it. But the situation they find themselves in is supernatural; there's a ghost in the barn, and the boy and the old man and the girl from across the tracks exorcise it in the course of the novel. It's funny, it's escape, it's supernatural. But I think it is very true, too, in the human relationships within it.

MARY RODGERS

Interviewed by Paul Janeczko

BOOKS BY MARY RODGERS

A Billion for Boris   Harper and Row
A Word to the Wives   Harper and Row
Freaky Friday   Harper and Row
The Rotten Book   Harper and Row

P.J.   How did you get started writing?

M.R.   I was orginally, and still am, a composer. I wrote a musical called *Once Upon A Mattress* and for a long time I didn't do anything but write music; but Broadway is very difficult now. It is very hard to get shows on, and I was one of the lucky few writers who was approached by an editor, instead of the other way around. Ursula Nordstrom of Harper and Row wrote me a letter and asked if I would be interested in writing a children's book and, since I have five children and the first songs I ever wrote were songs for kids, it's an area I'm familiar with and sympathetic to. I decided to try and the first thing I did was something called *The Rotten Book*, a picture book for kids, full of badness and wicked thoughts, and it put librarians off a little bit. Then I realized that the area I belonged in more truly was sort of young adult books, because picture books involve a minimum of dialogue, and what I love to do is write conversations. Next was *Freaky Friday* and after that, a sequel called *A Billion for Boris*. Now I'm working on another sequel to *Freaky Friday*. *Freaky Friday* is about a girl who wakes up one morning and realizes that she's turned into her mother. The new book is about how the boy and his father, in the same family, change places. That's what I'm working on now.

P.J. How do you get your ideas for books? *Freaky Friday*, in particular? How did that idea come to you?

M.R. It really did come from the fact that I had a very boring childhood. I'm probably too strong to call it unhappy, although at times it certainly was. I was frustrated all the time by the fact that adults could do what they wanted to, it seemed to me, and I never could. I had a rather strict mother, and I was convinced that she was having more fun than I was. I think I was right, as a matter of fact. Lately, when I talk to kids and ask them if they think their parents are having more fun than they are, they don't necessarily think they are; and I think that's because there's a greater degree of truth between parents and children now than there used to be. Grownups don't try to hide their unhappiness and problems from children as much as they used to. When I am thinking about a project, I try to think in terms of what I call "What if?" The "what if?" has to do, usually, with trying to make childhood a more bearable experience for people who, even one day at a time, might find it unpleasant—which is why I think my book seemed to deal in fantasy. I mean, in *Freaky Friday*, you're in someone else's body, having the fun of finding out what it's like to be a grownup. In *A Billion for Boris,* they have a television set that tells you what's happening the next day. I tend to think in terms of what kids would like to do if magic things could happen; then, from there, I write a rather realistic treatment of what would happen. They're not fairy tales in any sense; they just are based on one basic premise that is fantastic.

P.J. How long does it take you to write a book?

M.R. It varies. It's hard for me to tell because in both *Freaky Friday* and *Boris* I started the book and had to go off and do something else; in one case, I wrote a children's musical and in the other case I wrote a grownup book. But I work, I guess, two or three months. I have a peculiar schedule: I leave my husband and children and I go to a little cabin we have in the country, and I work twelve hours a day—which always shocks kids. They're appalled at the idea—it appalls me, too, as a matter of act. It's rather a dreary life, but you do get the work done, because there's nothing else to do up there. I work four hours, and then take a break for an hour, until the day is over. I walk around a lot; I think it's because when I was small—eleven or twelve—my parents were always sending me out in New York to get fresh air (which, of course, you don't get anymore, anyway). I used to carve out wonderful conversations for myself as I was walking down the street, just imagining wonderful daydreams and fantasies. I think that's where the thing of writing dialogue in my head started.

P.J. Do you write from your own experiences?

M.R. Oh, I think so—I think everybody does—but not literally. I find it difficult, for instance, to write in the first person in terms of somebody who isn't essentially me. And, as an exercise, I've been trying to do that because I'm rather outgoing and, I think, optimistic; but I also can get explosively angry (or would like to, if given the opportunity). It's harder for me to get inside the head of somebody who's shy and passive and keeps resentments hidden inside.

P.J. What other kind of writing do you do besides writing for young people?

M.R. Well, I write a column with my mother for *McCall's Magazine*, a monthly column called "Of Two Minds," that's interesting to kids to whom I'm speaking. Because my mother and I fought so viciously when I was a child, people are fascinated that we work together now. I think it's because I staged such a long-term, open rebellion with my mother that all of that anger is really out of the way now. We can disagree, but we have a very good working relationship and a good personal relationship. I do that and, for instance, I worked on *Free to Be You and Me*, a record which the kids know and love. I love it because it came about in such a wonderful way. Marlo Thomas went to Ursula Nordstrum and said, "I can't find any non-sexist literature; what'll we do?" She put Marlo in touch with me, and we sat down, and between us and Letty Pogrebin of *MS. Magazine* and Gloria Steinham, we contacted all of the people we knew who were well-established, talented writers—like Mel Brooks (they didn't have to be children's writers)—and asked them if they'd like to contribute to this project, and the response was remarkable. It was terrific. I wrote two songs for it, one of which I like a lot, based on "William's Doll;" the other I don't like very much. I sort of edited Shel Silverstein's story called "Ladies First" (which I would like to take full credit for, because it's divine) and helped put that whole project together.

P.J. When you are writing a book for young people, is theme a conscious effort, or do you merely try to tell a good story and let the theme surface on its own?

M.R. The minute I get the good "what if?" ("What if" you wake up one morning and find out you're in somebody else's body?) then, before I even start, I think, "What are the implications of that? What are the lessons to be learned?" Not in a preachy sense, because I like to write funny books. There are very few funny books written for kids, and it's the only kind I like to write, so I hope the messages, whatever they are, don't thud people on the head. It is incumbent upon writers for kids to have a theme that's kept in mind. I think that ought to be true of any author. It doesn't have to be a lesson; it's just that you have to know what you're writing about, what it is you're trying to say. In my case, it almost always has to do with relationships between grownups and kids, which I think need constant examining and opening up and bettering.

P.J.   What do you feel you owe your readers?

M.R.   I guess an understanding of adult mentality, more than anything else, even though I think there's a much greater degree of truthfulness now between grownups and kids. I think grownups tend still to be very protective of their own bad feelings, of their hurts, their sensitivities, their shortcomings; and, first of all, I think it gives the kids a very unrealistic view of what it feels like to be a grownup. Secondly, if you set yourself on that kind of pedestal, you're hurting the chances for communication. I always tell my kids, for instance, if I'm in a rotten mood, "Listen, I'm in a rotten mood, so look out. It has nothing to do with you, but I'm really jumpy today, so don't make trouble." I wish people had said that to me when I was little. I always thought it was my fault. And I reacted negatively and, pretty soon, I was in trouble.

P.J.   Was there a particular person who influenced you or inspired you to become a writer?

M.R.   Well, I think Ursula Nordstrum, for the simple reason that it hadn't occurred to me to try it professionally. I'd done magazine articles, on request, things like that; but, just as it is in school, when you find that you're doing terribly well in physics or French, or whatever, you begin to get interested in it because somebody has confidence in you. I think I began to be inspired by the confidence Harper and Row had in me, as much as anything else. You like to do what you do well.

P.J.   What would you do if you were not a writer?

M.R.   I'd be a doctor. Which is a great source of frustration. I, in fact, spent a great deal of time in the Presbyterian Medical Center a few years ago to see if there was any paramedical work that I could get involved in that would be interesting; but, unfortunately, that kind of work is not creative medicine; it's mechanical. I guess the other thing I would love to do is write a Broadway show, if someone came to me with a wonderful project—but I am not about to go looking for one.

P.J. What advice would you give to young people who want to become writers?

M.R. Don't try huge books. It's too easy to get discouraged. Start off with short stories. When I talk to students, they will tell me, "I started this story, and I am now on page seventeen and I don't know how to end it." Obviously, by this time, they are bored to death with the whole thing. I tell them to establish small goals and work—do it all the time. Read. Stay away from the television sets, and dip in and out of a thesaurus. I discovered, for instance, that one of my kids who is twelve didn't know there was such a thing as a thesaurus, and he had gotten to the point in English compositions where he couldn't think of any more words to use. He didn't know there was such a wonderful thing as a fount of extra vocabulary.

P.J. Do your own kids write? Do you encourage them to write?

M.R. Not aside from their academic work, simply because they happen to be slightly unusual as they are both professional singers with the opera, so they don't have very much time left. What I do encourage them to do is to write "thank you" notes, since "thank you" notes are something you have to write anyway. They are nice to write and you might as well set yourself the challenge of seeing how interesting and how much fun you can make them. I've always told my kids to pretend they were actually having a conversation with whomever that was and then clean up the grammar and spelling later. That's the way I started, and I began to get compliments on my "thank you" notes when I was about eight or nine, and I guess that was the seed to something. I thought, "Well, at least I can do that."

BARBARA WERSBA

Interviewed by Paul Janeczko

BOOKS BY BARBARA WERSBA

A Song for Clowns   Atheneum
Amanda Dreaming   Atheneum
The Boy Who Loved the Sea   Coward-McCann
The Brave Balloon of Benjamin Buckley   Atheneum
The Country of the Heart   Atheneum
Do Tigers Ever Bite Kings?   Atheneum
The Dream Watcher   Atheneum
The Land of Forgotten Beasts   Atheneum
Let Me Fall before I Fly   Atheneum
Run Softly, Go Fast   Atheneum (Bantam)
Tunes for a Small Harmonica   Harper Junior Books
    (Dell)

P.J.   How did you get started writing?

B.W.   Well, Paul, actually, I've been writing all my life; I started to write when I was a very small child. I was always writing, but I didn't know I was a writer. It took me until I was about twenty-seven years old to discover that I was a writer and should be a writer. Up until that point, I had been an actress, and had a very difficult life. I had not been very happy in the theatre, and when I was twenty-seven, I went away to Martha's Vineyard and wrote a book. The next year it got published, through incredible beginner's luck, and so I left the theatre and went into writing full time; that's what I should have been doing right along.

P.J.   Were you a writer in school? Did you write for the school?

B.W.   It was the only thing I did well in school; I was terrible in school. I don't know how I got through school. I was not interested in anything but English, and I wrote well and I read well. But I was terrible in math, geography, sciences, and languages. I think the only thing that got me through school was that I wrote very well.

P.J.   Where do you get the ideas for your books? How do you decide what to write about? Are they from your own life experiences?

B.W.   I don't really decide what to write about; it decides to choose me, I think, rather than I decide to choose it. Usually, ideas and characters come to me very strongly out of my own life. Everything I write is very personal, and when a story or place or character takes over very strongly, and demands that it be written, then I usually know there's a book there. I cannot fabricate a book; I cannot decide to make up a book. It is always something that has to come to me as an idea, very strongly.

P.J.   Is theme a conscious effort on your part, or do you first write a good story and the theme fits into that naturally?

B.W.   I think the latter is true; I couldn't start with a theme and then write a story around it. I would find that very peculiar; I always start with the story. But you find that if the story is strong enough and true enough, there's always a theme underlying it; it always has something more abstract to say than the story itself. But I don't think any good writers look at theme first; I think they look at the story first.

P.J.   What is your writing routine like? How long do you write? How long does it take you to write a book, let's say, *Tunes for a Small Harmonica?*

B.W.   Well, *Tunes for a Small Harmonica* was a wonderful book to write. It took eight months, which is a very brief time for me, and then I rewrote it several times. I've spent as little as six months on a book. It very much depends on the book. But I write everyday of my life, and since I've become a teacher, I tell my students that they must work for a certain number of hours every day. It's essential; you just can't sit down when you feel inspired to write. You have to go to your desk everyday as a routine.

P.J.   Whether you're inspired or not?

B.W.   Whether you're inspired or not. Whether you feel well or not; whether you are tired or not. It seems that the routine is more important, in some ways, than the writing.

P.J.   Do you write for a certain amount of time each day?

B.W. I write for a certain number of hours each day, including Sunday, and sometimes Christmas; although this Christmas I did not.

P.J. Can writing be taught?

B.W. That's a hard question, because I've just started to teach writing. It can't really be taught, but you can guide people who have talent and help them avoid terrible mistakes. The mistake they always seem to make is that young writers don't wish to write out of themselves; they want to write what they do not know. So my job as a teacher, I think, is to teach young writers to write only what they do know, to write out of their lives, and not to work for style. Style is a thing that comes out of who you are; style is your personality.

P.J. What about craft?

B.W. Craft takes a whole lifetime to learn; one is never finished learning craft. Craft is the vessel that enables you to get out into the waters of the material. Craft is the boat you have to ride to get into the interesting waters of the material. Every writer's craft is a little different, but it's a lifelong process; you never come to the end of it. Often, you have a story that you want to tell and you don't know how to tell it because you don't have the proper craft; you don't have enough craft. And the word "technique," which is a confusing word, is, I think, simply a way of using the tools of craft. The tools are the same for all writers, but the way each writer uses the tools becomes the technique. So you will find that Hemingway will have a technique different from Updike, and Updike will have a different one from Norman Mailer. Each person has his own technique.

P.J. What is the essence of good writing?

B.W. Well, the first words that come to my mind are clarity, simplicity, a beauty of language; an ability to use the tools well. Just as a piano player uses each single note of a piano well, a writer uses each word well.

P.J. Your latest book, *Tunes for a Small Harmonica*, is a departure from your other books. Any reason? Did you grow into that departure naturally?

B.W. It is such a departure that I don't know where it came from, and that's always what you say when you have a book you like very much. It seems to have written *you* rather than your having written *it*. It was a terrific departure for me because it's very funny and I'm not a terribly funny person. Many of my books have been sad. I was on vacation, supposedly, when this book came to me. The first words of this book just started coming to me, so in the midst of my vacation I started to write a book about a tomboy named J.F. McAllister, who falls in love with her poetry teacher in a New York school and gets into terrible trouble because of it. But it's a book that came to me; I have no idea where it came from, and maybe that's what inspiration is. Inspiration is a very fancy word, but when a book takes you over and the characters start doing their own thing, then you feel inspired.

P.J.   How do you know when a book is done?

B.W.   I don't know how you know, but you do. I used to, in the beginning, make very copious outlines of books, and that began to stifle the books themselves. I was sticking to the outline rather than letting the material take over. I find now, after about seventeen years of writing, I just write little notes all over the house to myself about the book I am writing. I write on the blackboard in the kitchen, and on the backs of envelopes, and I do a very rough, subconscious kind of outline. The book tells you when it's finished, when it has resolved itself as best it can. I've always known the beginning and end of each book I wrote, but never the middle.

P.J.   How do you know when a book is not ready? When it's not good?

B.W.   When it dies on you. Often you will start to write a book too soon, before it has germinated inside you, before it has begun to build up a life inside you, and it dies on you. It sticks its feet stubbornly in the middle of the road; it won't go forward; the dialogue gets very uninteresting and artificial. When you find yourself bored with your own book, you're in terrible trouble because, to work alone every day, you have to be fascinated with your own work. If you find yourself bored and getting up to get a cup of coffee every other minute, something is wrong; the book isn't ready yet.

P.J.   What do you owe your readers?

B.W.   I think I owe my readers exactly what I owe myself, which is interest in the book because I'm the first reader of every book I write: fascination, interest, suspense, most of all a desire to turn the page, to keep on going with the story, and the story is people.

P.J.   Can you think of specific writers or perhaps people in your own life that have influenced you to become a writer, or influenced you as a writer?

B.W.   No one I knew personally ever influenced me to be a writer. In fact, when I was in school, no one ever noticed that I was a born writer. But other writers have influenced me tremendously: the poetry of Yeats, Pound, Rilke, Eliot; the novels of Virginia Woolf; especially the works of Carson McCuller; though I don't write in any way like her, but she was a good friend of mine and I love her books. So I have been inspired mostly by the people I've read; never by anyone I've known, which is funny.

P.J. Do your books contain poetry?

B.W. I always sneak it in.

P.J. Are you a frustrated poet?

B.W. I'm not a frustrated poet because I write so much poetry for myself but, as you know, poetry is very hard to get published. I have published a child's book of prose poetry called *Amanda Dreaming*. I think poetry is the source, is the beginning, and I make my students write poetry even though they say they can't because it's the essence of language and clarity and brevity. It's my favorite thing, poetry.

P.J. What advice would you have for young people who want to become writers?

B.W. To do it everyday. You can always divide the writers from the nonwriters by seeing who does it every day. It's just like practicing the piano every day. I noticed since I just started to teach last summer that my class fell into two halves: those who wrote every day, and those who kept putting it off and waiting until they were inspired. If you find a young person who will write every day for himself over a period of years, I think you know he is going to be a writer. Because it's very lonely and it's very hard, and nobody is asking you to do it; and there's a very small chance of getting published when you're young. So the persistence is the thing that makes a writer.

P.J. In two of your books, *The Dream Watcher* and *Run Softly, Go Fast*, you portray young people whose family life is not particularly happy. Does that reflect your own upbringing? Your own experiences at school, let's say?

B.W. I'm sure there are a lot of happy families in America, but I don't know too many adolescents who are satisfied with their family life; there must be some, somewhere. I certainly was not. It wasn't the fault of my parents, but my parents were divorced when I was twelve. I lived with my mother and visited my father, and there was certainly conflict there. I don't think I had a terribly unhappy childhood, but you know it's very hard to write books about happy people, because they tend to get dull; and if you look at fiction as a broad genre, you will see that it's mostly about unhappy people and how they solve their unhappiness—how they work through it. There have been very few great heroes in fiction who have been happy people. They would not get written about if they were. You know, the Hamlet fiction or the dissatisfied people. My childhood was not any unhappier than anyone else's but there's something in the art of fiction that deals a great deal with unhappiness.

P.J. Why did you go into the theatre, and why did you get out of the theatre?

B.W. I think I went into the theatre because I wanted to be loved. Very few actors will say that, but I think it's true; and as I know many actors, and I'm involved with actors, I think it is a terrific desire to be loved and noticed. Acting is a very childish thing; it's a showoff kind of thing. Actors are terrible showoffs. I always thought that actors wanted love and writers wanted recognition. I don't care if I'm loved as a writer; but I do care about the recognition, that the books be appreciated, and that they reach somebody. If I had had a better sense of myself as a child, I would have gone immediately into writing because it's the thing I enjoy. I did not like to act. I was never comfortable on the stage; it was too public. The thing I like about writing is that I do it alone, at my own leisure.

P.J. And you left the theatre to write.

B.W. I was in the theatre for fifteen years. I started as a little girl and stopped when I was twenty-seven. I must say I never missed it, once I stopped acting. I never looked back. To this day, when I go to the theatre, it's all very unreal. The funny thing is I am about to have a play produced on Broadway this year, God willing, and I will be back again in the theatre, but as a playwright this time, not as an actress.

P.J. Could you talk a little bit about that play?

B.W. I could talk to you two days about that play, but for the purposes of this brief interview, many of the young people who are hearing this tape, I think, have read *The Dream Watcher*; and five years ago, I turned *The Dream Watcher* into a play for an actress named Eve LeGallienne, who is now seventy-eight years old and will be playing the old lady in the book and the play, *Mrs. Woodfinn.* This play has gone through a five-year nightmare of producers and options, directors and disasters. It had a tryout performance in the summer of 1975 in Connecticut, which was very successful and now it's been optioned for Broadway. But so many terrible things can happen to a play before it gets to Broadway that I can't speak about it before then. But it has been an interesting experience because very few people get a chance to work on material the second time. I loved working again on *The Dream*

Watcher and taking it one step farther, of developing the characters more, of putting it into a new form. It was a great pleasure to work on that book again.

P.J. Do you have a favorite book that you've written?

B.W. Yes, I do have a favorite book; and just as mothers love their homeliest child the best, I love my book *Let Me Fall before I Fly* the best. Not just because it didn't sell, but because I feel it is more representative of me. It's a book that had a very small sale, because it's extremely abstract and strange. I love it very much because I feel that it represents me better than any book I have written. It's a very short little book about a child who makes friends with an imaginary circus, a tiny little miniature circus. But it's funny to love that one the best, because nobody else loves it except me, really.

P.J. How does Barbara Wersba see the world?

B.W. Well, it keeps changing. I think in the past ten years or so, I tend to see it very darkly; that's why some of my books are quite sad, for example, *Run Softly, Go Fast. The Dream Watcher* is sad in many ways. I think I've always tended to see the world too darkly, to see a sadness and suffering, which is why, as I've told you before, I love *Tunes for a Small Harmonica,* because it is a funny book, and it has a certain crazy joy in it that I like. I'm going to be forty-five this August and I keep thinking it's about time for me to see the world a little more lightly and have some fun before I get old.

P.J. Do you plan to do more humorous books?

B.W. I would love to do more humorous books if they would come to me; as I said, books come to me—I don't reach out and get them. I write what comes to me strongly and keeps knocking on the door of my mind. It's much more pleasant to write a funny book than a sad book, because you find yourself laughing at the typewriter and having a cheerful day for a change. I would like to write another funny book, except you can't be funny on purpose; humor comes naturally, or it doesn't come at all. One cannot decide to be funny.

P.J. When you write in your daily routine, do you write at a typewriter?

B.W. Yes. Well, I'll tell you a funny thing. When I write poetry, I write in longhand because the typewriter is just too noisy and large to compose a poem. When I write fiction, I write completely on the typewriter.

Interviewed by Paul Janeczko 95

P.J. Do you spend a lot of time rewriting?

B.W. I spend too much time rewriting. I'm one of those people who cannot write a sentence without crossing out every word and going back and doing the sentence over. It is very rare for me to write three, four, or five pages without constant corrections. I find when I do dialogue I can go much farther without changing; I can spin along with dialogue. But with narrative, I'm always tripping myself up by correcting and correcting and correcting. But each sentence to me is like a brick wall going up, and if some of the bricks are weak, I can't build the wall. So my writing process is very slow.

P.J. Why is the dialogue easier for you?

B.W. Because the people start talking in your mind if they're good characters—like the ones in *Tunes for a Small Harmonica*. They begin to talk in your mind and you just type as quickly as you can to get them down because they're having this conversation in your head. The narrative is harder because that's you inventing that. I wish I could write in a sloppier way and correct it later, but I seem to be overly perfectionistic; as I'm writing on the page, I begin rewriting. I leave very fat margins and keep writing in ink on the typewritten page.

P.J. Then when you have all those corrections made, you correct?

B.W. Yes. Then I go back and type two or three pages over. I can only do, I would say, a maximum of three pages a day on the typewriter.

P.J. And how long will that take you?

B.W. A whole day is six or seven hours, so you can see how slow a process that is; I also work out loud, and unless it sounds right to my ear, I can't go on to the next page. The structure must seem strong before I can go on to the next page, because I don't know what I am building on. Those bricks have to be solid, though I know writers who work in a much looser way, and I think they have more fun.

P.J. But you'll spend six or seven hours every day writing?

B.W. That's right.

P.J. And sometimes have three pages?

B.W. That's right. If I have three pages to show for it, I'm very lucky. But I must explain that I get up and get coffee; and I might turn on the radio or have a cigarette; or the phone, unfortunately, rings a good deal. I find some of the best work I do is at four in the morning, because that's one of the quietest times I have. So much of my work is done before dawn, to get away from the telephone, which is a terrible nuisance.

P.J. What things should a young person who wants to be a writer be aware of?

B.W. The first thing he should be aware of is himself. The very first thing he should notice about himself is whether he likes to read. I am positive you cannot be a writer unless you are a great reader. When kids tell me that they want to be writers and I ask them if they read and they say, "Not very much," I'm very suspicious, because you can't really want to be a writer without being a passionate reader. So, the first thing you have to do, if you want to be a writer, is learn how to read well, and read diversely—not just stick to the things that interest you. Go far afield. Read everything; read as much as you can; read all the time. The second thing, as I mentioned before, is to write every day, even if it's only an hour or two; even if it's only keeping a diary or a notebook, do it every day. The third thing that's useful is to have one person you trust to whom you can show your work. I have been very lucky in the last fifteen years in having one friend who, I think, is a great critic; not my agent, not my editor, but just a good friend. If a youngster has one older person, hopefully an English teacher he trusts, it is good to show his work. You know, writing is so lonely to begin with, that it's very nice to have someone at the end of the day to show your work to and get a little feedback on it. So the things I would suggest are first, to read; second, to write every day; third, to have one person you trust to show the work to; and fourth, not to think about publication. One can't just think about publication; it gets you confused. I know kids of fourteen and fifteen who have sent a lot of work out to magazines and manuscripts to publishers, and it has been a very futile effort. The first thing to do is learn how to write. If you are any good, you will be published. I have a kind of crazy faith that good writers will always get published, no matter how the work gets to the publisher—if it's tossed over the transom, as they say, or if it's left at the door of the publishing house—I believe that good writing gets published, but it takes a certain heroism to be a writer because you do it alone and it's hard and it's lonely; and most writers make very little money. I think perhaps there are one hundred writers in America today who make a living at it; everyone else has another job or a spouse to support them. It's a very brave thing to be a writer, but it's also very exciting and the reward of having a book published is very great to your morale and to your spirit.

LAURENCE YEP

Interviewed by James Duggins

BOOKS BY LAURENCE YEP

Child of the Owl	Harper and Row (Dell)
Dragonwings	Harper and Row
Seademons	Harper and Row
Sweetwater	Harper and Row (Avon)

J.D. We are chatting with Laurence Yep, author of *Dragonwings*, one of the honor books of the Newbury Prize. Maybe you could tell us something about what it's like to write a book that gets a lot of attention.

L.Y. Well, it's fun; it's nice going around meeting people and talking to them about things you've written. But basically, I always think this attention is incidental to what I write; for me, the writing is more important. It's a way of living in some ways, and it is a very intense kind of activity. I mean it's more than just hiding away from the world. In a way, it's remaking the world, trying to change it, and taking in a bit of the world and making it your own and putting it out again in that world. Specifically, things I hear about other people or people that I meet go into my mind and somehow they come out on paper in a different kind of situation that I have set up, and then that book goes out. For instance, in *Dragonwings*, a lot of the characters are based on people I know, or about things I read, but none of the people or things I read blended together in one group; it was my own mind that put it together.

J.D. You were going to tell us something, too, about how you started writing, since you did start in high school.

L.Y. I had an English teacher that took some of us aside and told us if we wanted to get an "A" in his course, we had to get something accepted nationally. None of us did, and he took back that threat. But I was bitten by the bug, and I kept on writing; when I was a freshman at Marquette, when I was eighteen, I sold my first science fiction story, and I started writing science fiction professionally. I got four rejections for every acceptance. I took a lot of hard knocks in a way. I had editors and publishers tell me I couldn't write, but I kept on. Then a friend of mine wound up at Harper and Row and she knew I wrote science fiction. She suggested I write some science fiction for young adults and children and I wrote *Sweetwater* and, eventually, I got into *Dragonwings*, which is about Chinese-Americans.

J.D. When we talked earlier, you spoke about the fact that, more than money, writing books gave you a chance to look at yourself differently. You talked also in the same way about science fiction. Can you tell us something about that? What do you mean, "to look at yourself differently"?

L.Y. I was born in San Francisco and was raised in a predominantly black ghetto and went to school in Chinatown. All the books that I could find in the library didn't really deal with my own kind of experience. They were about boys and girls on farms, or they were about neat little ranch houses in the suburbs. The closest things that spoke of things and experiences that I was having I found in science fiction, e.g., when they talked about aliens and when they talked about strange new worlds and what was happening there. What I was going through was in science fiction, and I got into reading a lot of science fiction. So it was natural to write science fiction. As a matter of fact, that first story I sold was about a time when California sank into the sea and this young man survives the earthquake and subsequent flood and comes back looking for his own roots in San Francisco—and San Francisco is underneath the water.

J.D. That is how you started, really. Another thing that you said— and I think a lot of people would be interested—is that your father is not a neurosurgeon, that you are not a rich kid who simply lolled around and had nothing to do. What does your father do?

L.Y. Well, he's a postal clerk now; but we used to own a grocery store, and I used to have my own chores in the store. My parents were pretty good about it; they would let me work my chores around my writing time and, of course, I had to do my homework, too. I had to work a certain amount of hours each day in the store because it was a family-run business. We didn't have much in the way of luxuries or anything like that. It has been pretty much hard work, in a way.

J.D. So you really could work your own way through and, at the same time, establish a craft in writing. When were you paid for your first story?

L.Y. I was paid for that first story when I was eighteen, and I got a penny a word. It took me about six months to do, and it was $90. It sounds like a lot until you consider how much time I had to put into that story—over six months. But I kept on with it. A lot of the time with writing is learning to live with rejections and with the fact that publishers and editors aren't always the most intelligent people. At least you can feel that inside.

J.D. What does your father think of you now, about being a writer?

L.Y. He is very happy about the kind of attention I am getting but, to tell the truth, he has never read anything I have written because he is not very much of a reading-type person. The thing that I respect about him is that he has always been very supportive that way. As a matter of fact, not many of my family have actually read what I have written. They accept the fact that I have gotten some attention and that I am trying to make my living as a writer, but they think it's a chancy kind of thing. I think they would prefer I have something that is more dependable.

J.D. The fact that you don't go to a job everyday—does that create unusual conditions for you, e.g., that you get up and you don't leave the house?

L.Y. It's a matter of discipline, in a way. With me, writing is addictive; if I don't get to write at least three or four times a week, I start getting very angry with people and very annoyed. For me, writing is really a pleasure that I seek out actively, and I try to set out a certain number of hours for it, and my family knows not to bother me. I have a special area where we live to do my writing. I sit down there and look at my typewriter and things start coming. But it took a long time to get there, because it's not an easy thing to suddenly forget that you are sitting at your desk by a typewriter, and that your bedroom wall is in front of you, and that you are really on Mars or some far-away world among alien kinds of creatures. That's why it's important, I think, to have special boundaries that you set around yourself, special times, special places, special situations where your sense of the world breaks down and your imagination gets to come out.

J.D. Do you write and rewrite and rewrite, or do you do it just the first time and somehow it comes out the way it's going to be?

L.Y. Well, I have heard of writers who get it out in just one draft, but with me, it's a very painful process. I do about three thousand words a day, and every book I do takes about three or four rewrites. Since each novel goes about sixty or seventy thousand words, it takes quite a bit of writing. As a matter of fact, I no longer remember the exact plot of my first children's science fiction novel, *Sweetwater*, because I had to do so many rewrites on it. There are a number of characters I cut out and I changed the sequence of events around. Writing is a long, painful process; and it's a growth kind of process where you come to terms with yourself, I think, and you learn a lot about yourself because, when you write, you can rework a lot of the problems. If you are angry with someone, you can take it out in your writing. You may not publish it, but at least you get it out someplace, somewhere, and you have given vent to it. My father came over from China when he was eight, in the twenties, but he never liked to talk much about those days because a lot of unpleasant things happened. He is not the kind of man who likes to talk about what he has gone through. But I have always wanted to imagine what it was like, so part of that got mixed up with *Dragonwings*. *Dragonwings* is a story about a Chinese-American aviator who flew back in 1909. I read a newspaper account of that aviator; I copied it, and kept notes on it and it was very easy to visualize the scene of that flight. But trying to explain why that aviator was on top of that hill, flying that airplane, was a whole other problem, and it took several years to explain it. The way I eventually did it was to tell it from the point of view of the son, who was about eight when he came over from China.

J.D. There are great descriptions of the earthquake itself, and the way the people responded to the earthquake in San Francisco. One of the things I would like to know is, when you describe the way the family pushed this ancient, creaking plane up the hills in Oakland, in order to ultimately fly it, how did you get the experience to describe that? How did you know what the wheels felt like touching the ground, and the way that the plane itself sounded leaving the ground? Probably, we have never been in a plane that small or that ancient.

L.Y. Neither have I. Part of that is a science fiction technique, and people misunderstand me when I say that and they think I am inventing it, and I am not. You are taking things you know, and you are placing them in another situation. For instance, when you talk about the sounds that a wagon might make. I'm thinking about the times when I wheeled piles of boxes into the store on a creaky hand truck, pushing at things; and my father and I have flown kites. He makes very beautiful Chinese kites. Also, you can hear the flap of clothing when you are on a hill and it's very windy. It doesn't take that much to imagine what the canvas on an airplane wing will sound like. It is that kind of a situation where you take things you know and apply them to a situation you don't know.

J.D.　Where did you get the idea for that marvelous Red Rabbit, the horse?

L.Y.　At that time, I thought it was the God of Wars horse, and I have since read another account that says it's somebody else's horse; but that comes from research, from reading a lot. When I did the original research on *Dragonwings*, I didn't do it with the intention of writing a book about him. It took about four or five years after I had read the article on the Chinese-American pilot to actually finish the book. Of course, I was doing other things at the time, but it took a long time for it to come out.

J.D.　I loved the book, and there were some parts of it that were really insightful for me; I learned things that I had never really thought about, and I saw things in a different way. But asking you, as a Chinese-American, and discovering some turn-of-the-century atrocities toward Chinese people, how did you feel? Was it outrage? Was it sadness?

L.Y.　Well, when I first read about those kinds of things, I felt angry; but the kind of writing that that anger produced wasn't very good, it wasn't very readable. I learned that anger is a good thing to get yourself set up for writing, but after a while, you have to put it aside and adopt another perspective. Also, the fact is that when I did more research I found that the Chinese themselves, back home in China, weren't all that innocent when it came to persecuting minorities.

J.D.　You mean your own minorities?

L.Y.　Yes. Their own minorities in China. It seemed to me that the real problem was prejudice and stereotyping people; and no matter what race or what culture was producing those stereotypes, there was prejudice. So it was a question of working around them. I had grown up in America thinking about myself as a white American, and I didn't really face up to those kinds of problems until I went back to Milwaukee, Wisconsin, where I went to college for a few years. All of a sudden I was in the middle of a predominantly white American community. And while nobody came out and painted slogans on my wall or spat at me, yet I felt a difference. Trying to explain that difference, I got into all these other things, such as trying to work on an identity for myself. If I wanted to think of myself as a Chinese-American, it would be like looking in a mirror and seeing only a mask;

and if I took off that mask, all I would see would be no face underneath the mask. And the mask would be out of a Hollywood prop room: I could be a Chinese laundryman; I could be a Chinese houseboy or any kind of stereotype that comes out of the movies. So while I was trying to work around those stereotypes and come up with some positive images for myself, it wasn't done out of anger. There is a kind of perspective you get out of being angry and sad, and you are dealing with something basic because you are creating a self.

J.D. You said earlier that the process of discovering yourself in writing makes it more enjoyable, even though there may not be much financial reward. Do you have any advice like that to young people who would like to begin to write seriously, who might like to plan to make a living by writing?

L.Y. It's a long, hard process, and you have to be willing to live with a lot of rejection, I think. Your ego has to take a beating. I can show them a number of rejection letters I have gotten that ought to have made me stop writing. Certainly, if I had gone into writing, planning on making a living, it wouldn't have worked. So they have to keep on writing, and they have to realize that even though they may feel great about what they write, objectively, it may not be that good at first. It may need more reruns; they may have to rewrite that same scene four or five times before it will be interesting enough.

J.D. Larry, how many other books besides *Dragonwings* have you written?

L.Y. I have written two other children's books: *Sweetwater* was out before *Dragonwings; Child of the Owl* was out after *Dragonwings. Child of the Owl* is about a little girl growing up in Chinatown back in the sixties who has spent most of her life outside of San Francisco. Something happens to her father, and she has to go to live in Chinatown for the first time in her life. She finally confronts being Chinese, because she has never had to think about it before. But living in that kind of situation has forced her to reasssess herself. I also have done an adult science fiction novel, *Seademons,* and I have plans and projects for others. But it has taken about ten years to get to the point where I am doing those kinds of things and, certainly, the first seven years were very lean and hungry ones.

J.D. You talked about *Dragonwings* being a Chinese-American book. And these others you have written. Do you think of yourself as a writer of ethnic novels? Is there such a thing? What is an ethnic novel?

L.Y. It's ethnic in the sense that it is based in some culture that has differences from other cultures around it. But I think if a book is good, it ought to be read by anybody from any culture, because it is going to be about people basically—people who are angry, people who are in love, who are dealing with different kinds of situations. If it's a book that has to rest purely on an ethnic basis, that is, it is about a certain culture and it's about certain kinds of problems that are confined to that ethnic group, then only people who belong to that ethnic group are going to read it. I like to think *Dragonwings* can be read by other groups also. I hope almost anybody can imagine himself as an eight year old boy coming over to America, because I have tried to write that book in that way, to make them see and hear and feel what that boy is going through when he first comes to America.

J.D. Since some people still have concern about it, in *Dragonwings*, you used the word "demons" and, even though you are careful to explain it in the book, what's the objection to the word "demons?" What are people responding to?

L.Y. People have objected to the idea of using demons because they think of demons and devils; and I mean it in another sense, e.g., demons are like genies or elves—they can do good or evil to a person. So I was using it in that sense.

J.D. As I recall, "dragons" too has that kind of connotation in your book. Do people seem not to carry the language further than where they are, as a consequence?

L.Y. Well, actually, it's just an accident in English that "demon" has a lot of evil connotations. In its original sense, it was a creature who could do good or evil. Socrates, the philosopher, had a demon (a daemon) who drove him on to do good; and it was only when the writers of the New Testament began trying to translate Aramaic into Greek that they used demon in the sense of the devil. As for dragons, they do more good in Chinese culture than they do evil; specifically, they bring rain, they can bring luck, they guard treasures as well, but they can be friendly. It's not just the sea that has dragons, but it's every body of water—even a little tiny wishing well can have a dragon in it, including a palace and servants, inside this well. I was trying to work with some Chinese myth and folklore, and bring it out in an American situation, because, sometimes when you read folklore, it seems very far away and it doesn't seem to apply to your life; but when you find dragons and demons just around the corner, I think that is something else again.

J.D. Larry, you work so hard on a book—for months or years, writing and rewriting—and suddenly you have a book like *Dragon-*

wings that's successful. Where would beginning writers start? Say, students in a classroom in Topeka, Kansas? What should they do today if they think they would really like to become writers?

L.Y. The basic kind of thing is to read a lot, to find out what past writers have done. There are different ways of setting up a character. You can set up a character by the way he looks, by the way he dresses; you can confine it just to the way he talks without ever describing him. There are any number of ways of doing that, and the only way you can find out about that is to read good books, and find out how other good writers have done that. Once you start picking up on these little techniques, then you should write about what you know. Write about your own high school; write about your class; about your teachers; write about your family. That's what I did. The first rejection slips I got were on stories about my friends and family, but I learned from them. You learn from your mistakes, and you go on from there. Of course, you have to be willing to experiment. You have to be willing to try a lot of different types of stories until you find your own kind of voice. It takes a long time before you can develop your voice, and the good writers that I know personally all have a good sense of craft; that is, they know what past writers have done, and they have tried to imitate those writers that they admire. Through that process, they developed their own voices. But it took a long time before they got there.

J.D. Writers are funny people, in general. They are people who want to be alone, who want to sit by a typewriter or with pen and ink someplace much of the day, and keep working and working on sentences and paragraphs and chapters and books. Do you think that it is within that process that you know what you are doing? Is it the science of it? Is it an inspiration? Or what?

L.Y. I once knew a man who wanted to write, and he was convinced that the only way he could do it was by having correct grammar. He went through any number of books on rhetoric on how to write paragraphs. So he had a sense of craft, and yet he would not actually commit himself. He wouldn't put himself into those words; he wouldn't go beyond a certain stage. I think you have to get to a point where that sense of craft just becomes part of your unconscious; you just do it without thinking. You put these words down on paper in a certain way without really thinking about it because it's just natural to you. But it's a long time before you get to that stage.

J.D. You work, and work, and work.

L.Y. I sound gloomy about it only because most of the kids that I have met have an idea that writing involves someone sitting at his desk and, all of a sudden, this light bulb appears over his head, and he writes the Bible in one hour. It just doesn't work that way. It's a long, sweaty process, and it really is emotionally exhausting.

Laurence Yep

PAUL ZINDEL

Interviewed by Paul Janeczko

BOOKS BY PAUL ZINDEL

Confessions of a Teenage Baboon   Harper and Row
     (Bantam)
Effect of Gamma Rays on Man-in-the-Moon Marigolds
     Harper and Row (Bantam)
I Love My Mother   Harper and Row
I Never Loved Your Mind   Harper and Row (Bantam)
My Darling, My Hamburger   Harper and Row
     (Bantam)
The Pigman   Harper and Row (Bantam)
Pardon Me, You're Stepping on My Eyeball!   Harper
     and Row (Bantam)
The Undertaker Went Bananas   Harper and Row

P.J.   How did you get started writing?

P.Z.   Well, actually, the first thing I ever wrote was a collaboration
with another kid when I was in high school; we decided we really wanted
to work over a geometry teacher whom we hated. We decided we would
write in the local newspaper a short story called *The Geometric Nightmare*, in which we depicted this teacher as being the monster that he
was, very much like the character of Laurence Olivier in *Marathon
Man*, except our teacher did it with geometry. I also found out that
when we did that, we turned into celebrities within the school; it brought
us a lot of attention which we didn't get in any other way. We weren't
exactly the best basketball stars in the school, and we seemed to have no
other talent; but we found out that by writing some of the most

provocative, funny and stinging things that we could, it brought a lot of attention which, I suppose, is also the way Dorothy Parker wrote.

P.J.   Now, despite the fact you took this geometry teacher to task, you, yourself, became a teacher.

P.Z.   Right. I didn't notice it at the time, but there are a lot of us who go through our lives doing nothing but staying in school, and school happens to be a pretty terrific place for some of us. Some kids have parents who beat them; some kids have parents who never understand them. In fact, in most of my books I always paint the parents as being ogres and inconsiderate people. I paint them in very blank terms or as ciphers because, as far as I'm concerned, most kids like to prefer that their parents don't exist. This happens to be, I think, a part of the way kids really contribute what they can to civilization. They're meant to rebel; they're meant to ignore their parents; they're meant to totally change, and, in that manner, they invent the new, and it is the new that presents the method by which civilization takes a step forward. So I find the phenomenon very legitimate, and because I write books with kids in mind, kids are my audience; I speak to them and, therefore, I have to make my parents as they see them. They really prefer to ignore them or fight with them or get into enormous conflict with them. They don't tend to give their parents a full shake until later on in life when they've already formed themselves and are no longer threatened as to what their own character will be.

P.J.   Where do you get the ideas for your books? How do you decide what to write about?

P.Z.   I was a school teacher for ten years—a high school teacher—and I would sit in the back of a study hall (which was my work assignment), and some of the kids during those periods would throw pennies and M&Ms at various teachers; but I found it much easier to let these kids, who were usually the troublemakers in the school, just come up and tell me their problems and their stories, and I never really passed any judgment. They would tell me about abortions they had, or breaking and entering, or funny things like setting off firecrackers in the bathroom or smoke bombs in a movie theatre. Everything seemed to have a demonic quality; but I found it rather inventive, to tell you the truth, and I found the stories honest, and I just never passed judgment on them. It also prevented them from throwing pennies and M&Ms. They like to talk to strangers, to anyone other than their parents, as a rule.

P.J.   How long does it take you to write a book?

P.Z.   The actual writing of a book would take about three months. The living of the book, the collecting of the information, the thinking out of the scenes, the planning of the scenes, the technical elements of it, take about a year. A book of mine, *Pardon Me, You're Stepping On My Eyeball!*, has material in it that I had to research in Florida and California, so I spent a year in those two states. I just jotted down all the notes I could find, and I stopped off at all the places I thought kids would like to stop along the way. At one point, I bought a firecracker—fire rocket—that was supposed to go something like eight hundred feet in the air and explode in the shape of an American flag, and I set that off in a state where it was illegal, but I didn't know it. They usually sell those things on the borderline of South Carolina, but I set it off in North Carolina. And then they have things like monkey farms and freak farms, and all these things that any kid would like to go to see. I would just take notes on these things. Ripley's *Believe It or Not* they love down there. California has a whole different type of culture that is very freaky, and I used a lot of that material in this book.

P.J.   What is your writing routine once you have your research done?

P.Z.   Sheer laziness, but I try to force myself to write about two hours every day, if I can write. I'll tell you the truth—I don't force myself at all. I actually wait until the material is ready to come out. I have a certain list of rules that I set for myself. Number one, I make sure that what I am going to write about is real, based somewhere in reality. If I'm going to have a scene where two kids are going to understand each other, have a moment of understanding in Arlington Cemetery—as in my new book— I, in this case, went to Arlington Cemetery and looked at the grave sites. I went to John F. Kennedy's grave and saw the way the torch was set up. If I didn't have the real location I was using, I would go to a cemetery that was on Staten Island or somewhere around, that I could research it in, and then I would bend that reality to fit the necessary fiction. There was an English teacher at a high school where I taught who made it his assignment one day to have all the students go to a graveyard and lay down on a grave and write whatever thoughts came to them for an English composition. That was a rather horrific assignment, and I think he got a lot of complaints from the parents. The kids thought it was sort of logical, though.

P.J.   What other rules do you have for writing? You mentioned this set of rules before.

P.Z.   I think every writer gets one quick shot. Every kid that ever lived could write a terrific first book, and in my case it happened to be a play.

Interviewed by Paul Janeczko   109

But after that, if you're going to be a professional writer, you have to learn, I believe, techniques of structure. If you don't you really have to suffer under a lot of rewrites, and the chances are you're never going to fulfill a book. A lot of people, a lot of kids included, can write very interesting short compositions, but in order to get a full-length book, you have to have your main hero go through a series of crises that pay off in a very complex answer. In the case of kids, you've got to use highly-charged language; you have to collect things like graffiti. In this new book, I have the lead character, Marsh, starting off making a list of the things he hated most. Every day in class, he would make a list of those ten things he hated. He hated Mrs. Zucker, who's teaching his class, because she wears crooked eyebrows and talks like she's using reality as a crutch. And he'd hate the kid in front of him because he's got "ring around the collar." They like a lot of highly-charged, funny things that they recognize from television, from their own graffiti that appears on walls that are their own expressions; and, yet, they don't like to be talked down to. You have to sort out those expressions which are going to pass and date you as being an adult talking down to the kids. You have to sort them out from the kinds of expressions that you know are going to be around for ten, twenty, fifty years, and that's hard to do.

P.J. What is the essence, then, of good writing?

P.Z. Good writing, I believe, follows some set rules. There has to be a set basis of structure. Usually, it involves a protagonist and an antagonist, plus a third person who's involved in a climax. Most people want to identify with the protagonist, and that protagonist has to be taken through that lead character; that main kid, if you will, has to be taken through a series of adventures and conflicts and challenges, each getting worse than the others. Usually, you can call them traps, and you see this in *Huckleberry Finn*, and you see this in *Tom Sawyer*—a series of mounting traps that the kid has to face and eventually conquer. Involved in that is suspense; but there is a most crucial element that a kid should look for in reading a book to find out whether the book really is offering anything new or is trying to rip him off. That happens at the end, when the protagonist suddenly finds himself—that kid, the lead kid—in a situation where he has to say, "Hey, maybe there's something wrong with me. Maybe all these people that are attacking me are attacking me for some reason," and, at that point, there needs to be one other requirement. That requirement is that the author provide a solution, an insight to that character which lifts the reader's own insight, so that he himself learns something from reading the book. That makes

Paul Zindel

the difference, I think, between a good book and a good writer, and what you might just call a "pot-boiler." It makes the difference between a terrific book, a book that adds something to humanity, and a book that is just exploiting and trying to get the kid's buck.

P.J.   Is theme a conscious effort on your part, or do you merely set out to write a good story and theme becomes a part of it afterwards?

P.Z.   I think the professional writer is aware of theme, aware of structure, aware of scenes; extensive notes and research are all taken ahead of time and then you must forget them. Then you have to allow the subconscious to operate and to allow all that material that you jammed into yourself to operate as though it were the influx of a day's activities. I know a girl who is thirteen years old who plans her dreams for the night. She likes to be kissed by boys. Usually, before she goes off to sleep (by the way, she's considered not very bright in school) this not-very-bright girl knows enough that if she thinks about a problem or a situation prior to going to sleep, she will dream about it. And there is a connection between dreams and writing, and the idea is to allow enough of the technical basis to be there, but still permit the dream mechanisms and the imagination and, what teachers often yell at kids about, daydreaming, to operate. Writing is primarily daydreaming; good writing is daydreaming with a technical basis.

P.J.   What do you owe your readers?

P.Z.   Well, one kid wrote me and said he wanted seventy-five cents back because he hated my book; so in that case I owe that kid seventy-five cents. But I refused to send it to him because I decided he didn't really read the book. He goes to the library and copies down all the authors' names and he sends them cards saying, "I read your book, and it's lousy. Send me back seventy-five cents." I feel he is now a millionaire. What do I owe my readers? Actually, I don't owe them anything because it's all automatic. I am honest with them; I have used the professional rules I mentioned to you before; I've used honesty in talking to them; I have also selected the kids honestly as my audience to whom I'm speaking— now those are the major things I owe them. If I start talking to kids at the beginning of the book and really hook them into something that they can relate to, and then suddenly in the middle of the book decide I'm ashamed to be writing for the teen-age mind or the teen-age market, that what I want to write for is adults, and I suddenly do a switch and try to become philosophical and in a very lofty manner that goes above their heads, then that's delinquent of me, and it's pretentious of me.

Interviewed by Paul Janeczko   111

That's why all my titles—like *Pardon Me, You're Stepping on My Eyeball!; My Darling, My Hamburger; The Pigman*—are ones which I market-test with the kids to make sure they are things they want to hear, that I'm telling the same information, but on a level that makes it interesting to them. For instance, I was bored to death by Shakespeare during high school. I think it should not be taught in high school except to those few kids who are probably born of very rich parents and have an extraordinary background in English to comprehend it. I had to wait many, many years before Shakespeare meant anything to me. Right now, I owe the kids honesty and, with that, I receive their approval in return. I receive critical approval, and receive all the things that fine writing, honest writing, can bring; so it's kind of not something you owe them—you owe it to yourself as much as to them. Otherwise, you're a flop. The world recognizes honesty in the long run, and that's the only way you survive as an artist.

P.J.   Is there a specific person who influenced you, who inspired you to become a writer? Besides that geometry teacher, I mean?

P.Z.   Yes, there's a phenomenon that goes on in writing, when you're a young kid, particularly. You find someone that you think is your mentor, is the person that's most influential to you. It usually is someone that you meet in person. In my life it was Edward Albee and Sloane Wilson and a few other famous people who came to Staten Island, and I was exposed to them. The phenomenon is rather strange, because what you do is begin to talk to these people in reality and find out they are not anymore special. When you meet a person like that— who is successful in a field—you realize, "I can do it, too." So the most important thing that can happen to a kid's life is to meet someone in an area of his interest who encourages him, who takes a few moments to show him that he's a human being, too—that there's a certain amount of work one has to do and a certain amount of training and, if you want that, then go for it. There is nothing like personal contact with someone successful in the field of your interest that can get you going. I must also add to this that the kid will eventually be rejected by the true writer, by the talented person, because he won't have time for him in the long run. He'll accept a few moments of his time, but in the end, usually, your mentor will give you a good swift kick and you'll be on your own, which is kind of the whole story about adolescents anyway, isn't it?

P.J.   What advice would you give young people who want to become writers?

P.Z. Well, if they want to become writers, and they are aware of that, then they should be aware of the fact that they are (what I consider writing) neurotic. It's a neurotic compulsion from within. Kids that already know they want to be writers—fiction writers—know that they want to live in dreams more than they want to live in reality. They have visions they want to express on paper more than in reality; and I'll tell you I would advise them, more than anything, to be careful not to live too much in their dreams, because the real life occurs outside of books. I think they should be careful to maintain an immersion in the real world, as well as in the fictional world. I think the kid who is the bookworm, and the kid who pulls himself away from sports and does not look at a well-rounded life, can be in trouble. So the kid who has a talent for writing, who has what I call a neurotic disposition towards it, I think has got to make sure he is balanced, which is one of the current themes of dreams. The dreams of kids usually are to compensate and to give you clues about what is missing from life.

P.J. One final question: How does Paul Zindel see the world?

P.Z. I asked a few directors, if I were to play an acting role, how would they cast me. Ask your friends, "If I went into movies or television, what role do you think I could play?" Right? Well, one actor told me, "You could be an absent-minded professor, or you could be a mad scientist." I thought those were two very good roles that I wouldn't mind playing. Then someone came along and said I could be an angry student that appears in Chekhov, who is a little complicated and very boring—unless you get a little older and feel like looking at something that doesn't have much plot in it. I see the world pretty much as the critics tell me I see it. I see it as a place without any Santa Clauses; I see it with no Easter Bunnies; I don't wait for any tooth fairies to pop quarters under my pillow; I see it as a place where you really have to get out there and help yourself. I see very little magic about it; I see a constant revelation of science making humanity more aware of itself, more aware of how the human mind functions. I see childhood becoming less of a mystery, and adolescence being less of a mystery. I find the world rather exciting from that element. It's very hard to live in a world in which you believe in nothing. So, I suppose, for me, I see myself, more than anything, needing something to believe in and, at the moment, I think I believe in some of the rather basic beliefs of religion. I don't mean those connected to believing that there's just one God, or any of the orthodox religions; I see some of the values of religions and how they came to be, and I think they are coming back again, along with a new President, actually.